DON'T
KILL HIM!

The story of my life with Bhagwan Rajneesh

Reprint 2019

Published by
FiNGERPRINT!
An imprint of Prakash Books India Pvt. Ltd.

113/A, Darya Ganj,
New Delhi-110 002
Tel: (011) 2324 7062 – 65, Fax: (011) 2324 6975
Email: info@prakashbooks.com/sales@prakashbooks.com

facebook www.facebook.com/fingerprintpublishing
twitter www.twitter.com/FingerprintP
www.fingerprintpublishing.com

For manuscript submissions, e-mail: fingerprintsubmissions@gmail.com

ISBN: 978 81 7234 444 3

Processed & printed in India

DON'T KILL HIM!

The story of my life with Bhagwan Rajneesh

A memoir by
MA ANAND SHEELA

FiNGERPRINT!

Bhagwan Shree Rajneesh
(Osho)

Bhagwan Shree Rajneesh, perhaps the most controversial Indian spiritual guru till date, is counted among the most influential figures of the twentieth century. He set up His first major ashram in Pune, and later moved to the US, where His followers established a commune in Oregon.

Named Rajneeshpuram, this commune was spread over 64,000 acres and was like a city in itself, housing more than 5,000 residents by 1985. Over time, it developed its own urban infrastructure, complete with fire departments, a transportation system, a police station, shopping malls, a water reservoir, a sewage-disposal plant, a post-office, a well-staffed security force, and even a 1,300-metre-long airstrip.

Till 1990s, Bhagwan was a bigger controversial figure than a major spiritual guru. Though He enjoyed a massive international following even back then, His irreverent discourses and ideas, rumours about drug addiction, and His general disregard for laws and religions ensured that He had many critics and enemies everywhere, particularly in India and in the States.

His espousal of freer sexuality alarmed religious leaders in India and popularized Him as "Sex Guru." Later in the US, He earned the sobriquet "Rolls-Royce Guru" as He indulged in His desire for luxury cars and collected close to hundred Rolls-Royces in less than five years. He reportedly had a penchant for luxury watches and pens as well and spent hundreds and thousands of dollars of donation money on them.

When Rajneeshpuram dissolved in mid-1980s, Bhagwan was indicted on thirty-five counts—charges included immigration violations as well as making false statements on His visa application. At the same time, other Rajneeshpuram leaders, including Ma Sheela, were booked for much graver charges. These included attempts to murder public officials, setting an enormous wiretapping network, and plotting the first bio-terror attack on the United States. While Bhagwan was fined $400,000 and was deported from the country, some commune leaders were sentenced to many years of imprisonment. When nearly twenty-one countries denied Him entry, Bhagwan returned to His ashram in Pune in 1986, where He lived for another four years. A cardiac arrest reportedly killed Him in 1990.

Today, Bhagwan's official Facebook page has more than 750,000 Likes; His 650 books, available in 55 languages, have sold millions of copies worldwide; and His ashram in Pune still attracts 200,000 visitors annually from all over the world.

Bhagwan Shree Rajneesh perhaps was born great; in His life He achieved greatness; and after His death a greater greatness was thrust upon Him.

But no man is perfect. And great men like Bhagwan Rajneesh often have greater flaws.

I dedicate this book to my parents, Ba-Bapuji Ambalal and Maniben Patel, for bringing me into existence and instilling the right values in me.

I am grateful to my brother, Rohit Patel, for all the help and encouragement.

Thanks to Ma Anand Anupamo (Christel Hahn) for translating the text from German to English.

CONTENTS

Prologue

This is a book about my life and work with Bhagwan Shree Rajneesh. My loving father encouraged me to write it. It documents my experiences, my observations, my feelings and my life while I was working with Bhagwan as His personal secretary.

I hope this book serves to fill in gaps created by Bhagwan's disciples, who have so far eliminated all references to the period in Oregon from His biographies. To fully understand the man that Bhagwan was, it is important to examine His actions honestly and from all dimensions. As His secretary and a confidant carried out His every wish and command, I had the opportunity to closely observe His actions as well as the motives behind them. I was able to understand His grand vision and to see His immense talent, drive and awesome power. I also witnessed His manipulative side, His vengefulness, and His failings as an ordinary human being.

During my years with Bhagwan, I learned that the greatest of gurus can also be fallible human beings. I learned to separate their personality traits from their immense charisma and the power of their teachings. I also learned not to give up my integrity in the face of tremendous hardships, false accusations, and months of wrongful incarceration. I learned how to come through the worst nightmares without regrets, ill will, or blame.

The book begins on the day I decided to resign as Bhagwan's secretary and the operating head of the commune in Oregon. The first few chapters deal with the period immediately following my departure from Rajneeshpuram and the beginning of the legal nightmare manufactured by false accusations and trumped-up charges levelled against me by Bhagwan and His followers after my resignation. These were some of the most difficult and trying days of my life. I had never thought even in the worst of nightmares that I would have to live almost like a fugitive for doing so honestly and dedicatedly what I thought was my life's work. However, I did not have any regrets then, and I do not have any regrets now about this period, neither do I have any ill will towards any of the people responsible for this harrowing experience. I accept it as something that Existence wanted me to experience.

In part two, I pick up the thread from the beginning when I joined Bhagwan's movement around 1972. I had just turned twenty and had recently married my first husband Marc Silverman, who was later renamed Swami Prem Chinmaya by Bhagwan. In creating a new world of His vision, Bhagwan gave new names to people and places in order to erase their history and give them a completely new identity and meaning. In this latter part, I describe my experiences as a young Sannyasin. I detail how I got the opportunity to be the personal secretary of Bhagwan Shree Rajneesh in a short time, how I had the good fortune of having the chance of a lifetime to build an entire commune from ground up in Oregon—where over five thousand Sannyasins later worked together to bring Bhagwan's vision to reality—and how Bhagwan destroyed it in a fit of rage after I resigned from His service in the year 1985.

I saw Bhagwan extremely charismatic, brilliant, inspiring, powerful, and loving, and I also saw Him being ridiculously manipulative, vengeful, self-serving and hurtful. He disregarded all laws, moralities, ethics, and legalities of every community, society, and nation because He wanted to create a society of His own vision with its own laws and rules. I witnessed how He was at the top of His game in Bombay and Poona, how He gave shape to His commune, how He worked with people, how He manipulated the media by generating controversies, and what His grand vision was. I also observed His decline in Oregon which began with His dependence on painkillers and other drugs, and which ended with the ultimate downfall and dissolution of the commune in Oregon.

I loved Bhagwan and trusted Him implicitly, blindly. I've a deep and abiding respect for His teachings and remain His loving devotee even to this day. I remain grateful for the opportunities that He gave me, opportunities to work so closely with Him and learn so much from Him. I try to live by the lessons I learned from Him and the values He taught me. I urge the readers to dwell not on the scandalous and juicy tidbits of my story but on how my love for Bhagwan and His teachings helped me face all big and small challenges that came my way in life.

I'm also very grateful to my parents for their love and trust that sustained me through the most difficult period of my life and for their encouragement thereafter to live life in love and service. I'm particularly indebted to my father who introduced me to Bhagwan and His teachings. Since coming out of the US prisons, for the last twenty years of my life, I have dedicated myself to the memory of my parents through caring for the mentally, psychologically, and physically handicapped in my two nursing homes located in the outskirts of Basel, Switzerland. The nursing homes have been named after them as Matrusaden (Mother's Home) and Bapusaden (Father's Home). I would also like to express my gratitude to my family, particularly my sisters and brothers who have supported me unconditionally throughout life, and to my late husband Dipo (real name Urs Birnstiel; renamed Swami Prem Dipo by Bhagwan).

Finally, a word about my use of the words "love" and "Existence." Often when I've said that I fell in love with Bhagwan or that He is my eternal lover, I have been asked to define this love. What I felt for Him cannot be explained. Whatever it was, it was complete and whole. This feeling had no boundaries, no limits. It was the opening of an infinite horizon. Everything melted into these feelings and these feelings melted into everything. Freedom was their basis, and freedom was their end. Sex did not have to do anything with this feeling of love, but then I would not have refused sex if He had demanded it. Our every glance, every touch was devoid of sexuality, yet it was totally filled with passion. Anything and everything that happened out of this feeling of love was absolutely all right, perfect. This love had its own clarity and awareness, as one cannot experience in ordinary life. It opened a deep understanding in me. It was the highest state of my being. It consumed me. This love is still there. It is not of this world. I cannot stop it. It is just there. It is forever—a plan of Existence (or Nature or Universe or *Brahmaan* or whatever you may call it), and I am proud and grateful to be part of this plan. I will not exchange this love for anything in the world. I can even go back to jail for it. It knows no end. And I don't know when it began.

ONE

The Man with
the Inexplicable Life

There was once a man named Mojud. He lived in a town where he had obtained a post of a small official, and it seemed likely that he would end his days as Inspector of Weights and Measures.

One day when he was walking through the gardens of an ancient building near his home Khidr, the mysterious Guide of the Sufis, appeared to him, dressed in shimmering green. Khidr said: "Man of bright prospects! Leave your work and meet me at the riverside in three days' time." Then he disappeared.

Mojud went to his superior in trepidation and said that he had to leave. Everyone in the town soon heard of this and they said, "Poor Mojud! He has gone mad." But, as there were many candidates for his job, they soon forgot him.

On the appointed day, Mojud met Khidr, who said to him, "Tear your clothes and throw yourself into the stream. Perhaps someone will save you."

Mojud did so, even though he wondered if he were mad.

Since he could swim, he did not drown, but drifted a long way before a fisherman hauled him into his boat, saying, "Foolish man! The current is strong. What are you trying to do?"

Mojud said: "I do not really know."

"You are mad," said the fisherman, "but I will take you into my reed-hut by the river yonder, and we shall see what can be done for you."

When he discovered that Mojud was well-spoken, he learned from him how to read and write. In exchange Mojud was given food and helped the fisherman with his work. After a few months, Khidr again appeared, this time at the foot of Mojud's bed, and said, "Get up now and leave this fisherman. You will be provided for."

Mojud immediately left the hut, dressed as a fisherman, and wandered about until he came to a highway. As dawn was breaking he saw a farmer on a donkey on his way to market. "Do you seek work?" asked the farmer. "I need a man to help me bring back some purchases," the farmer explained.

Mojud followed him. He worked for the farmer for nearly two years, by which time he had learned a great deal about agriculture but little else.

One afternoon when he was baling wool, Khidr appeared to him and said, "Leave this work, walk to the city of Mosul, and use your savings to become a skin merchant."

Mojud obeyed.

In Mosul he became known as a skin merchant, never seeing Khidr while he plied his trade for three years. He had saved quite a large sum of money, and was thinking of buying a house, when Khidr appeared and said, "Give me your money, walk out of this town as far as distant Samarkand and work for a grocer there." Mojud did so.

As time went by he began to show undoubted signs of illumination. He healed the sick, served his fellow men, and his knowledge of the mysteries became deeper and deeper.

Clerics, philosophers and others visited him and asked, "Under whom did you study?"

"It is difficult to say," said Mojud.

His disciples asked, "How did you start your career?"

He said, "As a small official."

"And you gave it up to devote yourself to live as an ascetic?"

"No, I just gave it up."

They did not understand him.

People approached him to write the story of his life.

"What made you who you are today? How did you gain such knowledge?" they asked.

"I jumped into a river, became a fisherman, then walked out of his reed-hut in the middle of the night. After that, I became a farmhand. While I was baling wool, I changed and went to Mosul, where I became a skin merchant. I saved some money there, but gave it away. Then I walked to Samarkand where I worked for a grocer. And this is where I am now."

"But this inexplicable behaviour, it throws no light upon your strange gifts and miraculous achievements," said the biographers.

"That is so," said Mojud.

As nobody would speak of Khidr directly, the biographers created for Mojud a wonderful and mysterious history. As all saints must have their story, the story tellers constructed a tale in accordance with the appetite of the followers, far from the realities of life. That is why this story is not true. It is merely a representation of a life. The real life of one of the greatest Sufis.

(From *Tales of the Dervishes* by Idries Shah)

Bhagwan and my inner voice are my Khidr. Unconditional acceptance of this guidance has made me one with Existence. Existence has a lot to do with me and my life. I want to begin with a few very simple but profound words, which have become a part of my life.

Yes to Existence, to Life, Love, and Trust.

1
My Khidr had spoken

It was a morning like many others in the last months of 1985. I had no desire to wake up, because I was not looking forward to the new day. My body was sick and in pain. My heart felt heavy. My mind was filled with too many responsibilities. Work wasn't fun anymore; I no more enjoyed love and life. There was so much to be done however. I was the queen of the commune.

I did not even look forward to seeing the man whom I had loved devotedly for the last fourteen years and for whom I would have gone even through the tortures of hell without hesitating for a second: Bhagwan, my eternal lover, king of my heart. I had always felt I could never be without Him. He had considered me qualified enough to bestow upon me the enormous responsibility of managing the commune. On my own, let alone doing it, I would have never even imagined taking it up.

When I opened my eyes on this morning, I saw my beloved parents sitting on my bed. It was not usual for them to visit me this early. My mother told me her heart ached seeing me like this. My father looked disturbed and worried. They had come to know instinctively that something was wrong with their youngest daughter. They had always been very proud of me. Now they were spending sleepless nights because of me.

They had talked about me beforehand between themselves and had come to a conclusion. With tears in her eyes, my mother said, "If you do not change your lifestyle, you will soon be dead. You're a queen. You make sure that everybody has something to eat here. But for a long time you have not been able to enjoy your own food . . ."

With these words and their tears, my parents expressed their feelings about my way of life. Even I felt in my heart that something was seriously wrong. I had reached a point where I needed to make a decision. Love was my greatest and only strength. I could not let it become my weakness now. I felt I must change something in my life and that I must do it soon.

My parents had been living with me in the new commune for two years. The new commune was a great communal experiment in living a life of meditation to achieve Buddhahood, a safe place where Bhagwan's people could work and meditate together. Here they were not disturbed by the outside world and its people. Ordinary taboos and inhibitions could be brushed aside here. The only important thing was how to become Buddha. Here everything else simply disappeared from the mind. Money, power, and prestige were not operational here. The new commune was a place where love and togetherness formed the basis of existence. It was a dreamland created by Bhagwan. It was His life's work. And in His creation I was the boss, the queen. I was His personal secretary and the one in command.

A few days after my parents expressed their feelings about my condition, they left the commune to return to their home in India. Before flying back to India, they went to California to meet our other family members.

There were many communes worldwide. I regularly visited those in Germany, Switzerland, Italy, Spain, Denmark, Holland, and England. I flew to Europe every month. The European communes and Sannyasins were a much needed economic support for the development of Rajneeshpuram, our commune in Oregon.

A Sannyasin is simply someone who is prepared to give up everything and be initiated, someone who is prepared to walk on the path shown by Bhagwan. They are prepared to dissolve into Him with love. They're prepared to surrender to the highest freedom and be one with Bhagwan.

European Sannyasins had a quality of devotion and love for Bhagwan which I had not seen very often in others. I worked very closely with them, and we had a special connection. For the past few months, however, more than business trips, my trips to Europe had become my only chance to escape the pressures and demands of Rajneeshpuram. When in Europe, I felt somewhat removed from and not as exposed to Bhagwan's madness as I did in Oregon. There I was at a distance from the politics of Rajneeshpuram, the politics of Bhagwan. There I could breathe again.

On one of these visits, to Germany, I received an urgent call from Savita, my friend and assistant. Savita was a dear, loyal, and understanding friend, a devoted Sannyasin and a trusted colleague. She was competent and very efficient, and could take over my work in case there was an emergency. I had trained her for that purpose. Her love and devotion to Bhagwan made her my right hand. She was courageous, brave, and honest.

Savita took care of the financial needs of the entire commune, as well as those of Bhagwan. She was a trained and professional accountant and, at that time, she was the leader of our accounting department. In financial matters I never made decisions solely on my own; I always asked her for advice. I trusted her completely. She was a woman of high integrity. Never would she sell her soul for worldly comforts. Although she always seemed very gentle, she was very strong. I am proud to have had a friend like her. Even today I feel she is my soul sister, and I trust her implicitly.

In my absence Savita routinely took over working with Bhagwan. Between Bhagwan and me it was clearly understood that if something were to happen to me, Savita would replace me and carry on the work of leading the commune. I had recommended her to Him. Bhagwan had agreed with my choice.

Most people with whom I worked closely had a similar character. I did not want people around me who were greedy for Bhagwan and His views, or for enlightenment. For most of my staff, spirituality was not the main interest. They worked hard because they loved Him. They desired to learn from Him. They were ready to take responsibilities and work hard instead of wasting their time chasing dreams. They were ready to give everything they had in their hearts, without holding anything back. They expected nothing in return. They were dedicated to Him and His commune. This meant hard work without recognition or even acknowledgement.

During my frequent trips to Europe I constantly stayed

in telephonic contact with Savita and my other assistants. I always managed my work with them on phone. So while it was normal for Savita to call me that day, her reason for calling was very unusual. Savita was quite troubled and agitated and wanted me to return to Oregon immediately. Crying, she told me she had had enough of Bhagwan's madness and of His commune. I could immediately empathise with her. I was fed up too.

I flew back to Oregon the next day. I listened carefully to what Savita had to say. The problem was really nothing new. It pertained to His insatiable demand for more and more Rolls-Royces and expensive watches. Savita and I had been confronted with these demands nearly daily for a long time now. Now, however, we could no longer support it. We could no longer cover our distress by seeing the humour of the situation. It had gone beyond being a funny off-beat way of Bhagwan to make people see that there was no inherent value in such material possessions. It had begun to metamorphose into a nightmare. Bhagwan already had more than ninety-six Rolls-Royces and His countless brilliant watches were worth several million dollars. But He still wanted to have more and more of them all the time. His appetite for these luxuries was in fact growing, worsening. His demands for these no longer seemed merely idiosyncratic—they appeared to be the product of a deteriorating being.

Bhagwan's personal caretakers had also been giving us headaches. Because they were allowed to take care of His needs, these people behaved as if they had descended from the heavens. They made all kinds of demands in His name, without any shame or hesitation. They wanted better imported equipments for everything; quality material available locally was never good enough for them.

So it was the same old story: Bhagwan wanted to order more Rolls-Royces and expensive watches. Only, this time, Savita and I were no longer prepared to go ahead with it. During my flight back from Germany, I had come down with a bad cold, and since I wanted to avoid infecting Bhagwan with it, it fell on Savita to visit Bhagwan and work directly with Him. We were always very careful with these things; Bhagwan already did not keep very well. Going to meet Bhagwan by herself did not trouble Savita, because I was still physically nearby. In my presence, Savita as well as other members of my team always felt they were protected and in good hands.

In the following hours, my anxiety grew. I became more and more unhappy and had to do something to be able to be joyful again. Openly, I spoke about this with Savita, Vidya, and a few other trusted co-workers. But talking was no solution. Actions had to follow. I was ready for it. Finally, I said: "I will leave Rajneeshpuram. It has to be. If I don't do it, I will die. Geeta, please write a letter for me."

Beloved Bhagwan,

I feel You should know what is going on with me. This time upon my return there was no excitement, infact a dragging. I feel better lately when I am away. Because of these feelings I had to be clear with myself and You.

I have been finding it very difficult to simply take responsability for this community and its liabilities. The situation has reached the desperation point in me. My joy and pleasure has disappeared to the point of leaving or at least looking for a change of worship.

There are other small solutions that come and go, but they seem insignificant compared to the situation on hand. I have not come across any other bright idea.

Please guide

Love

Sheela

12th Sept, '85

I sent this short message to Bhagwan through Savita. Many of my colleagues were as troubled as I was. They too had to look inside themselves and find out what they wanted to do in future.

Savita returned with Bhagwan's answer: I could go to Europe for some time to work there in different communes and continue to raise money for Him. This heartless message made Savita and me very angry. In this message we could only see His desire to raise more money from European Sannyasins. This recent attitude of His towards the European communes and Sannyasins was disturbing. We often tried to balance things by sending gifts in His name to them. Nothing was like before any more. He was simply no longer the same person. In all things He only saw money. Money meant more Rolls-Royces and more watches. His people, His commune, His vision, His dream, everything seemed to have been forgotten. Even His discourses were at times inconsistent. He had no respect for others anymore. His leadership and guidance had become limited to only how He could get more money. Something was not right. The heart was missing. The feeling was long gone. Previously, harmony was always recognizable in His madness, but now there was only madness and disregard. Compassion and love seemed to not exist in Him any longer.

To live in a European commune just to raise money was not what I had imagined for the future. In fact I had become rather tired of raising money. I just wanted to go away. I wrote again to Him, this time to express my gratitude to Him, and to return His diamond watch and an expensive Mont Blanc ball pen He had once presented to me. As His secretary, I had proudly worn these diamonds. They were crown jewels. They belonged to the crown and the position, and I wanted to forsake both of them.

> *September 13, 1985*
> *Beloved Bhagwan,*
> *I want to thank you for offering me one of the most gracious and absolutely educational opportunities in my life.*
> *With this letter, I wish to resign as your personal secretary with the same love and respect.*
> *In Love,*
> *Sheela*

Now it was up to Him to respond; it was His turn to become angry. He asked Savita, "Why does she do that? Who does she think she is? Where does she want to go? Is she not happy?"

Savita told Him what I had asked her to say in case He still had questions. "Sheela is tired. She simply needs to go away from here." This was the only reason. I wanted to escape that madness, be alone.

Everything around Bhagwan had multiple dimensions. There were never situations that were just black or white. The same was with my departure. It cannot be traced back to one or two certain events. It was related to the whole atmosphere around Him, which often caused ugly and unhealthy situations. These situations had become increasingly frequent, and more and more oil was always being poured into the fire by Bhagwan and some special Sannyasins who lived with Him in the Lao-Tzu House.

I was the heart of the commune and He was the soul, the inspiration. We were a team. But now, He had retreated in part from His role. The spirit of His teachings could no longer be felt. He had lost interest in us as a community. I was not prepared to take responsibility for His people and the commune all by myself, alone. I did not have any such ambition. Moreover, I no more wanted to deal with His constant, crazy demands.

For several months it had been clear to me that He and the Sannyasins living in His house were violating the fundamental teachings on which the commune had been found. I would perhaps have been able to live with Bhagwan's financial madness. But there was a much more sinister element pertaining to drug abuse active in His house. I was not prepared to compromise on this front.

Bhagwan taught awareness. Without awareness, both meditation and enlightenment are impossible. His commune should have been free of drugs. No dependence should have been tolerated, because all dependencies divert one from awareness. We had taken many precautions to prevent drugs from being brought into the community. We had drug-sniffing trained dogs on the premises and every visitor was checked for drugs. Apart from the fact that drug use was against our religious principles, it was also legally risky. It could have given the US government a golden opportunity to close down our commune and imprison Bhagwan. We knew adequately well that in the political world, it was common to plant drugs on members or workers of unwanted organizations in order to cripple them. Drug use and abuse in Bhagwan's own house would have been an opportunity sent by God for a government waiting for a long time for something to charge us with.

I did not know about this problem until Madhunad, Durga, and Homa drew my attention to it one day. Swami Madhunad, a thin, tall man in his mid-thirties, was the pharmacist of Rajneeshpuram. I had little to do with him. We met only when problems came up in his work. Ma Durga, a nurse, was the head of our health department. She took her work seriously and was very reliable. Ma Homa was the head of our legal department, the first formally elected judge of the city of Rajneeshpuram. She was very candid and direct, and possessed a good deal of common sense. Although not a lawyer, she knew American laws well. Her experience always proved very valuable to us. Her legal opinion was not coloured by the ego of a lawyer. She was a good candidate to take over Savita's as well as my work in case of an emergency.

The drug problem was extremely troubling for me. It made me concerned both morally and legally. If exposed, it could have gravely endangered the safety of our existence in the United States. What bothered me the most was that the people around Bhagwan did not understand the gravity of the matter clearly. They judged the risk far too lightly.

From the information and documents that were shown to me, it was clear that a massive abuse of prescription drugs was active in Bhagwan's house. Madhunad, Durga, and Homa told me that fifteen fictitious medical files were used by Devaraj, Bhagwan's personal physician, to prescribe, order, and store drugs for Bhagwan. When asked, Devaraj claimed that fictitious files were necessary to ensure the protection of Bhagwan's personal data.

All medical files are generally confidential. Thus I could not understand this special justification for the presence of the fifteen fictitious files. Under the names of these fictitious persons, more Valium was ordered for Bhagwan's personal use than it was ordered for all other members of our community put together, and there were three thousand people in the community. Devaraj gave me no explanation as to why so much Valium was required. Apparently, he had set Bhagwan on a daily dose of 240 mg of Valium. The pharmacist Madhunad assured me that no competent doctor would allow his patients to take so much Valium, because the body responds less and less with such a high dose. Consequently, the dose has to be increased consistently in order for the drug to have an effect. This can ultimately lead to a circulation collapse and death.

As if this was not enough, I also found out that large quantities of Meprobamat were additionally ordered using Bhagwan's fake files. This sedative was later withdrawn from circulation by the FDA because it was dangerous and life threatening. It was not to be taken in high doses. As few as eight tablets could be fatal. I was told that Bhagwan received a combination of Valium and Meprobamat routinely. My big "Why?" did not receive an answer either from Devaraj or later from Bhagwan.

Then I looked at Vivek's medical files. Vivek lived in Bhagwan's house. She received a morphine preparation as a sleeping aid and for migraine, and, for no apparent reason, larger quantities of sodium pentothal, a narcotic which is usually used only in surgical operations. When I insisted on explanations, Devaraj told me that she needed it to deal better with the separation from her mother.

All these facts posed a great danger for both Bhagwan and the commune. If we had such doctors, we did not need any other enemies. I tried everything in my power to make Devaraj understand the far-reaching legal implications that could arise if someone were to find out about the drug abuse. He proposed to burn the record cards. The three of us—Savita, Madhunad, and I—shook our heads in disbelief. It was a nightmare, and it seemed likely to worsen in its course. As if we did not already have enough legal and social problems!

In addition to all this, I also found out later through Madhunad and Durga that Bhagwan also ingested laughing gas for two hours every morning and afternoon. Naturally, they were disturbed by the large amounts of nitrous oxide ordered. Such excessive orders immediately resulted in investigations of our pharmacy by the FDA (Food and Drug Administration) and FBN (Federal Bureau of Narcotics). Again there were no reasonable answers. I was only told that the nitrous oxide was for Bhagwan. If something was for Bhagwan, nobody was allowed to question it—this was the attitude of the people in His house. All of them thought they were very special. I thought all of them were very stupid.

When I tried to talk to Bhagwan about these medical distortions, he responded indifferently. He offered me no assistance. He told me to inform Devaraj of all medical pros and cons of the drugs and to find a solution for the legal situation. He did not want to be bothered with such issues. He also told me, "Seela, you take care that these people with the sniff dogs do not check John, because he brings the ecstasy for Vivek. Ecstasy is a new drug. It makes Vivek happy and keeps her quiet . . . Then she troubles me less . . . John says that it is not dangerous, and he is a doctor . . . Do not worry . . . I will take responsibility if something happens . . ."

I tried to argue with Him; in vain! I tried to convince Him that He did not fully see the extent of the legal ramifications. He brushed all my arguments with: "You just follow my instructions."

Such a reply from Him was not normal. I saw a direct threat to the existence of our commune in it. Until now He had always supported me when I had concerns or problems, but now He had suddenly become indifferent. This was new. I could not accept it. This indifference was a sign that His interest in the commune had seriously diminished.

Of course I did not do what Bhagwan wanted me to do. Obeying Him in the ecstasy-matter would have been against His direct orders to me to protect His teachings and His commune. I was frank and honest to Him. I told Him with difficulty that I could not pass on these instructions to the guards with the sniff dogs. He did not insist and dropped it.

In addition to these serious matters, there were many other small events as well that contributed to my distress and disillusionment. I no longer wanted to participate in the game. I wanted to uphold my integrity and not compromise just to be able to continue that lifestyle. In the past I had heard of

Vivek's many suicide attempts using sleeping pills. Even at those times I had always inquired how she'd got access to so many drugs even though two doctors and a dentist lived in the Lao-Tzu House. When I tried to put a stop to it, Bhagwan's explanation was that she had already faked suicide several times even before He'd met her. Then He tried to calm me by saying, "People who make fake attempts at suicide never really kill themselves. They are cowards. They use the suicide threat as blackmail." In the past these statements would silence me, but now I had had enough.

I was ready to neither commit suicide nor witness one. I wanted to go away. My parents felt the same way. Continuing to live and work in Rajneeshpuram could have been fatal for me. I wanted to leave. I wanted to go somewhere where I could be alone and think about my life. I wanted to go on with my life, apply what I had learned from this man whom I loved so much. Bhagwan's reply to my letter contributed to my decision. He apparently had been unable to guess how strong my feelings were. He had not seen the extent of my dissatisfaction. He almost took me for granted. He thought it would be most difficult for me to forsake the fame and power I had been enjoying for years. He did not know that fame and power meant nothing to me. I was with Him only because I loved Him, and I did not want this love to become my weakness now. I had lived with Him because we had been a good team. But now the team spirit was broken.

My brother Bipin was visiting. He had a very special relationship with Bhagwan as well as with many Sannyasins. Bipin was a funny, loving man with a good heart, although those who knew him only casually tended to find his humour difficult to understand. Bipin had helped me find the land for our commune. He urged me to not leave. He said I could not do that to Bhagwan and His people. He was surprised that I wanted to give up everything I had built. He thought I was mad.

This was true. But my madness had its own reasons. Neither He nor anyone else could understand it. Even I could not understand it myself. I only knew that I must go away— away from Bhagwan and His people. That seemed totally irrational to others as well as to me considering that I had immense power, respect, and recognition as His secretary.

Sometimes, when such madness comes in my heart, I myself do not understand it. But in retrospect I see its meaning. It is the madness of the heart, not of the mind. It has proven to be correct all my life.

Nobody could dissuade me from my decision in the two days that I spent at Rajneeshpuram after returning from Germany. Many Sannyasins came to say goodbye to me. Many wanted me to think it over once more. On both sides there were floods of tears. I thought that these streams of tears would wash away the whole commune. But that was not to be the case. It was Bhagwan who, later, with His crazy allegations, pressed the button and flushed the commune down the toilet. The storm of emotions was so high that it was really difficult for me to go. But it was time; nothing could stop me. My Khidr had spoken to me: "Leave Rajneeshpuram and everything you have been doing and move on."

I flew with Air Rajneesh from Rajneeshpuram to Seattle. I started at 13:30, because my flight to Zurich was at 17:00. As is clear, I did not flee or secretly escape from the commune as was reported later. I had chosen a commercial airline; the tickets had been booked in my name through the Rajneesh travel agency. Everything was paid for by credit card. I had no reason to hide anything from anyone. I had carefully informed all our department heads and everyone who meant something to me before taking leave. I had even told Bhagwan's mother that I was going away. Someone wanting to escape secretly would certainly not have informed Bhagwan or His followers about it in advance, especially not in the commune where there was always so much gossip. If I had to conceal my departure I could have waited until I had something to do in Europe, and then disappear suddenly from the commune. The truth is that my departure was as honest as my first encounter with Bhagwan. I had not joined Him secretly when I had first met Him, and I saw no reason to hide my departure from Him then. I could also not go without saying goodbye. I'm a transparent person. Secrets or concealments are against my nature. I, as Bhagwan's most trusted secretary, the proud mother of the commune, and the responsible head of a large organization, officially informed the commune through a notarized letter.

September 13, 1985
Academy of Rajneeshism
P.O. Box 27
Rajneeshpuram, OR 97741

Beloved Ones,
Love.
I am leaving the area of Rajneeshpuram and therefore will no

longer be able to carry out my duties as President of the Academy of Rajneeshism. Please accept my resignation effective today.

Best wishes for the future.

His Blessings

Ma Anand Sheela

When I left, I addressed the assembled Sannyasins who had come to see me off: "Take care of your beautiful home. Don't let it go downhill just because Mother is going away for a few days. If you need me, you can always reach me. I've left my phone number with Geeta, and I will be regularly informing you of my address."

As is evident, I did not run away. There was no escape. It was a proud flight to freedom, into the unknown. I think of September 13, 1985 as an important day in my life. It was my personal Independence Day.

2
The Odyssey begins

When I arrived in Zurich, my husband Dipo, a Swiss, was waiting for me. Dipo was in charge of the Zurich commune at that time. I'd met him in early 1981. From our very first meeting there had been very special feelings between us. I was the only woman in his life to awaken his interest, because actually he was homosexual. We had a very sweet relationship. He'd send me champagne truffles, my favorite chocolates, every week from Zurich. He knew very well that they were my weakness. I liked to enjoy them after sex. Dipo was a very sensitive person. He was chubby, soft, and cuddly, just the right man on whose shoulder I could lean my head and forget the world. We had fallen in love in Monte Carlo during one of my European trips.

After I left Rajneeshpuram, he also decided to leave Bhagwan to live with me. I'd told him on the phone itself that I wanted to leave Bhagwan and had asked him to meet me at the Zurich airport. He was shocked, but he did not ask any questions. He simply said, "I have access to an apartment in Freiburg in which we can stay for three or four days. It belongs to a Sannyasin friend of mine. We can go there immediately after your visit to the Zurich commune . . . these people are waiting to see you." He loved me. He instinctively knew exactly what I needed. For him, the choice between Bhagwan and me was clear.

When we arrived at the commune in Zurich, some of the Sannyasins present were angry and shocked. It was obvious: they could not understand why I had left Rajneeshpuram. Their behaviour was a little awkward and strange. They had received a message from Rajneeshpuram to disassociate themselves from me. I also did not want to spend too much time there; I just wanted to say goodbye to a few people with whom I had worked closely and who meant something to me.

Within twenty-four hours, Dipo and I were thrown out of the apartment in Freiburg because no Sannyasin was to have contact with me or help me anymore. Anyone to show interest or sympathy towards me was to be thrown out of the commune just as quickly as I had been excommunicated. I was to be treated like a leper. I was to be emotionally amputated, weakened, and destroyed. To a certain extent I had expected some of that, but I had not anticipated such an extreme and ugly reaction and such a severe excommunication after so many years of loyal service.

My practical experience and common sense helped me in this situation. Dipo had very little money, and I had none. We had to pick up Savita and a few others who had also left Rajneeshpuram after me from the Zurich airport. So we rented a small bus and picked up these ex-patriots. I asked Dipo to look for a small guesthouse for us where we could stay for a few days until we found work and earned some money.

It sounds simple, but it was not. There were many problems. We were totally confused and were suffering a culture shock. The time change and jetlag after the flight were adding to our discomfort, while the life outside Rajneeshpuram was proving to be an extremely difficult experience for us. We knew how to behave in our own environment as Sannyasins, but we felt lost with outsiders in the outside world. It was not easy to live as ordinary people. None of us knew how to be just ordinary. But we did know how to work. However, we did not know how to work in the ordinary sense. Until now our activities had always been connected to Bhagwan and the commune. To live in a commercial society had always been unimaginable for us.

We found a cheap guesthouse in the Black Forest (a wooded mountain range in southwestern Germany). Savita and the others first slept for twenty-four hours because they were physically and mentally exhausted. After my departure, Bhagwan and His new management had harassed them. They had to undergo a complete body check, their baggage was ransacked, and some of them were even financially blackmailed and put under great moral pressure. They no longer knew whether they were dreaming or awake. This change was much deeper than ordinary dislocations. They felt attacked and robbed, that too by people whom they had loved and to whom they had devoted many years of their lives. I was sad. Such disrespect was neither appropriate towards us nor towards the ideals of Bhagwan with which we had lived for many years. When I heard what had happened to them, I cried—not because of us, but for the Sannyasins who had been asked to turn on us so viciously. They'd sold their souls in the name of enlightenment. I wanted to spit on such enlightenment.

I disjoined my mind from what was going on in Rajneeshpuram and busied myself with the emergency on hand. What should we do? Where should we go? How to pay for our food? It was not only about my own subsistence, I morally felt responsible for the twenty-five people who had also left the commune. I thought about their lives, hearts, and souls before tending to my heart and my soul. I waited impatiently for Savita to wake up. She and I had a constructive way of exchanging ideas and thoughts. Together we were able to solve every problem. I was also worried about Bhagwan. I had heard horror stories about what had happened after my departure. I knew that if I could only talk to Savita and understand the feelings she had when leaving Rajneeshpuram, I would be able to better assess what Bhagwan was cooking up in His rage.

I knew Bhagwan and how He had treated other Sannyasins who had left Him in the past. So I'd expected a heavy retribution, but I had not envisaged that it would be so dramatic and so pathetic. I had just thought that my departure would lead to exclusion and maybe even excommunication.

Bhagwan liked to keep His troops in control, and He had used me to tie them to Himself. I knew that He would not be afraid to feed their feelings and their minds with false ideas, and He would certainly know how to use my departure for His own purposes. Exploitation of emotions was His business, and He was good at it.

But before we were able to rest, reflect, and discuss things, somebody knocked on the door. It was the man in charge of the guesthouse. He was accompanied by two journalists. Apparently, right after my departure, an extensive hunt for

Sheela had been ordered. Bhagwan had used my departure to effect a big media spectacle. I had never guessed that I was worth that much attention as a news story. Although I had been in public view for a long time, it had only been as a representative of Bhagwan and His commune. The fact that the media was showing considerable interest in me and my departure was rather surprising for me.

Why had they not found me right away? I had not gone into hiding. I mean, I had walked around openly on the streets, had even driven back and forth between our guesthouse and the Zurich airport. Plus, my face was known worldwide. The two journalists proved to be our saviours though. My immediate concern about how to pay for the accommodation and the meals for twenty-five people was taken care of by them. During the next six weeks, until their exclusive report was published, they settled all practicalities for us. They kept us hidden, and transported us from one city to the next, as well as from Germany to Italy. They even took me to an island in the North Sea and brought me back. We were followed by press helicopters, running cameramen, and the like. It was a big, ridiculous fuss, but it brought entertainment into our unhinged lives. We now had enough humour and distraction to deal with Bhagwan's allegations against me and the "gang"—the epithet He was using for our group—which were being issued on a daily basis now. I found the monstrous accusations dreamt up by His crazy imagination both amusing and appalling. It was frightening to witness what that man was doing in His crazy, pathetic anger. He was regarding my departure as a planned mutiny!

I think that if only I had left Rajneeshpuram without

others following in my footsteps, He would have acted with more tolerance. But the fact that the entire management team of the commune had followed me was too heavy for Him to digest quietly.

But I had not asked them to leave. It was not planned, but spontaneous. The others were unwilling to work in a commune where I was not present to protect them. They did not trust the other seniors in the commune. They did not feel right about what was going on in the Lao-Tzu House either. The entanglements of the Lao-Tzu residents with the people from Hollywood especially made them uncomfortable. There were four or five Sannyasins who had come from Hollywood and had moved into the commune. Their specialty was money, not their ability to work or their meditative attitude. They had been invited into the commune because they could contribute financially. Bhagwan had said, "They are useless people . . . but use them for their money . . . take care that their egos feel satisfied . . ." The deal was simple: they enjoyed Bhagwan's attention, and Bhagwan enjoyed their money.

Due to all this, my staff, like me, had been expecting—not unreasonably—some real trouble. They had worked with me and were aware of all the insanities thriving in the commune. So, when I left, they quickly left too.

I was completely open in dealing with people with whom I worked. I wanted them to know every detail of my work and to feel they were a part of it all. They were all competently equipped to handle emergencies in case of my unavailability. I trusted them completely and felt secure in my position. I needed no secrecy in order to keep my power. If I had ever been asked, I would have had no qualms about handing over my post to someone better suited. All in all, we were a close-knit group with immense mutual trust. Many a time, Bhagwan had tried to create rivalries between Savita, Vidya, and me but had been unsuccessful. Eventually He had declared us—not inaccurately—an inseparable tripartite team. After my official resignation, Bhagwan offered the vacancy to three others: Savita, Vidya, and Homa. None of them accepted it. All three left and joined me. This was no mutiny, no rebellion—it was just time for us to go. In my journey with Him, I had reached a point at which I had to go a separate way. He had often spoken about this process in the past. For every disciple a time comes when he must leave his master. At this point there is no turning back, no compromise. My time had come, and so had the time of many others.

I was always happy when I could agree with Bhagwan. With my love for Him, I had spoiled Him without restraint. But when it was a question of my integrity, I was always unrelenting. Bhagwan was aware of this strength of mine. He had always thought highly of it. He had always given me the opportunity to talk with Him freely about everything. I could always tell Him if something was bothering or disturbing me. Respectfully, I could always tell Him my position, even if I was in disagreement. He always granted me this luxury. He knew I did not fight just for the sake of fighting or to show how smart I was. My questions to Him came from an honest interest to learn and understand. He was a friendly and patient teacher. He gladly took time to explain everything to me. He knew that I was willing to learn. He also knew my respect for Him and my high esteem for life and learning. I never felt forced to accept a false belief or His opinion on something. Unlike

Devaraj I would never have been able to say "He is my master and I will give Him any medication He wants . . ." just to show my devotion to Him. I was also far from the attitude of His dentist Devageet who once bragged to me about the totality of his surrender in this way: "Bhagwan is my master. If He asks me to set fire to His house, then I would do it even if He was sitting in it . . ." I found these people idiotic and stupid.

I had my own standards for right and wrong, truth and falsehood. I was not prepared to compromise for what I considered right. That is what I called integrity. And my integrity was always staunchly aligned with the welfare of Bhagwan and His commune. With me, it was always about whether the commune and its people were happy and healthy. As the Mother of the commune, I considered it my duty to offer maximum protection to its people. Before this, however, came my own values and my understanding of life and people. That's how I wanted to live. Though I was transparent with Bhagwan and absorbed His ideas and His way of thinking and working, I was not ready to sell my soul. I could not allow one of my great strengths—love—to become my weakness.

Loyalty has been one of my strong virtues in life. For instance, even as a young girl of eighteen, studying at a university in America, I fought adamantly against racial discrimination. At that time I was working as a waitress in a restaurant in Montclair, New Jersey, close to the university, to earn some extra money on the side like many other students. It was a nice restaurant that catered to a wealthy clientele. I did not know that it was customary there to discriminate against blacks. The staff managed this in a very clever way. They had set aside some undesirable and unused tables for black guests.

Even if the restaurant was not crowded, the black guests were led only to these tables. And if they wanted to sit at other tables, they were told that those tables were booked.

Once I was asked to serve at a table with black guests. I was given special instructions on how to deal with them. My boss ordered me to demand a tip of fifteen percent from them even if their bill did not exceed the amount for which it was customary to add such a high surcharge. My boss told me clearly and in great detail that he did not like blacks coming into his establishment. The restaurant was exclusive, and he wanted to keep it so. To ensure that the blacks did not come back, he took care that they had an inconvenient and expensive experience in the restaurant, since according to the law he could not refuse to serve them.

When he told me this, I could hardly believe his words. I quit my job on the spot and went home. I was angry and disappointed. The next day I went to the NAACP (National Association for the Advancement of Colored People) and told them everything. I also lodged a formal complaint against the restaurant and its management. Later I heard that my complaint had caused a lot of problems for my ex-boss.

So, even as a young girl in a foreign country, I had enough common sense not to compromise at the expense of basic human values.

As I have already said, I left Bhagwan because I did not want to be pulled into His madness and forsake the values important for me. As I will explain later, I even took thirty-nine months of prison term on myself for I did not want to betray Bhagwan or anyone else. I, as well as some other Sannyasins who had dared to act differently, even had the opportunity to be the prosecution's witness against Bhagwan once. But that was not to be my *gurudakshina*, my gift of gratitude, to the master who had taught me so much.

In Rajneeshpuram, Bhagwan was my guide. Now I had to look for a different guidance in life. I left my life to Existence. I decided to follow its guidance completely and without complaints. When I had left Rajneeshpuram, I had not known what I would be facing, but I was prepared for everything—the good, the bad, and the ugly. I had no idea how many obstacles and difficulties I would have to overcome. I did not know how many stormy nights were about to come. The only thing my inner voice told me was to accept everything with a yes. Again, my Khidr had spoken.

In His wrath at our "betrayal," Bhagwan came up with numerous hastily concocted schemes to harass us. The biggest among them was: He blamed us for planning and executing terrorist activities against the American government and the commune.

It is important to see that these allegations were raised only after our departure, and never before. If He had the impression that we were so evil, why did He let us go in the first place? Why did He not oppose or stop us when we were still there? Why did He not hand us over to the authorities? Why did He tell me to fly to Europe to raise money when I sent Him the message that I want to quit? Does this sound logical? Doesn't all of this sound strange and twisted? Don't these facts betray His original objective of building a commune where the New Man of His vision could live and thrive?

The whole range of false accusations began with the

trumped-up charge of a theft of fifty-five million US dollars. This sum changed every day and with each new report. Interestingly, this accusation was media's favourite since it involved a large sum of money and was easily quantifiable.

I can still recall how the world press hunted me for days and weeks before finding me in Germany on the island of Juist. My hotel was suddenly surrounded by press people and cameras. The locals enjoyed the spectacle. It was far more interesting than the normal tourism entertainment that they were used to. The hotel manager ran back and forth excitedly.

I was tired, both from the trip and from the emotional roller coaster I had been on since leaving Rajneeshpuram. My mind and body were exhausted. I had left Rajneeshpuram in order to be alone. But now I was again surrounded by maddening activity. Finally I decided to come out onto the balcony of the hotel and answer some of the questions of the gathered reporters.

They wanted to know where the $55 million were. I showed them my pockets and said, "Here." This was always the favourite question of the reporters. Even today, after so many years, I still have to deal with this question. Other things have been forgotten, but not the fifty-five million.

As I said, every day there were new accusations, new charges. The gates of Bhagwan's imagination had been opened. No facts, no justifications were necessary any more. Bhagwan seemed to have had lost control of His senses. He seemed to be blurting out whatever was coming to His mind, without any thought or discrimination, and nobody around Him was brave enough to check this madness of His. Soon He lost His credibility. Intelligent people had difficulties believing His lies.

Another accusation was the attempted murder of Bhagwan's personal physician, Swami Devaraj. This was completely ludicrous, unimaginable, and preposterous. He based this allegation on a dispute I once had with Devaraj regarding Bhagwan's medical treatment. It is true that I had found it difficult to trust Devaraj's medical ethics, but I couldn't kill or even attempt to kill him for this. I mean one often has disagreements in life, but one doesn't go around killing people for that!

Then there was another ridiculous accusation of poisoning 750 people in The Dalles, Oregon, with salmonella bacteria. Such a pointless and heartless action would not have served any purpose. The whole Rajneesh community was accused by the residents of The Dalles for causing this epidemic in Oregon. In those days, it had become almost customary to blame Rajneeshees for all disasters in Oregon as well as in other parts of the world where we were concentrated. I learned that the health authorities, initially, had written a report that the outbreak of the salmonella poisoning was caused by a lack of hygiene in local restaurants. However, after the charges were levied against us, the report was illegally modified. I must warn all my readers about the judicial authorities of the United States and their practices. Their accusations and allegations must be treated with great suspicion and apprehension. My experience has been that they are more interested in personal and political objectives than in delivering justice to the people they serve. To this day I hear about this false accusation being used as a fact in many government reports.

In September 1990 came the final and the most bizarre charge—that of conspiracy to murder Mr Turner, the attorney general of Oregon. This accusation was levied against us just as the statute-of-limitations period was about to expire. This was five years after I left Rajneeshpuram, and nearly two years after I was released from prison after serving thirty-nine months.

It is important to note that when this new charge was brought up, the attorney general was up for re-election. I seem to have possessed the talent of bringing a lot of valuable publicity to local politicians in those times. Hence, at election time I was always in great demand. This charge was also their vehicle to gain both publicity and sympathy. I had had many run-ins related to the commune with the conservative attorney general of Oregon, but the accusation of our conspiracy to murder him was sickening and went well beyond any logical evidence. It seems that once the conspiracy to kill Devaraj did not stick, a new conspiracy with a new and a more prominent target was conjured up to help Mr Turner get elected.

However, the most incredible allegation was, and still is, that I had run away with $55 million. This allegation has been a constant source of amusement for my friends and me. At times I've actually wished we had access to such a large sum at Rajneeshpuram, and that I had run away with it. My friends have even joked how this was the only instance in which I had proven my stupidity beyond doubt: I left without taking anything! Actually, there were many people who used to believe that everything in Rajneeshpuram legally belonged to me because I was its legal head and had invested so much hard work into making it a reality, that too without any pay.

The fact is there was never so much free money in the commune for anyone to steal. It required enormous hard work to raise enough money to support a large community. There was never anything left over in the reserve. Our image in the world's eyes was one of immense wealth, but this was only a superficial image, like the ones often created of Hollywood celebrities. I think I know how this sum of $55 million came into play in reality. A few months before leaving, I'd told Bhagwan that we had $55 million in debt. I wanted Him to know this so He would stop demanding more and more money from me for cars and jewellery.

He asked me how these debts had gotten accumulated. I explained to Him: "We have obtained that much in lines of credit. We have spent more than $11 million for your Rolls-Royces, $8 million for watches and jewellery. Also, every month we need more than a quarter of a million dollars for your household and other expenses. Four million was the cost of construction of the Krishnamurti Dam. Twelve million we raised for the festivals and two million for Avenue Bhagwan . . ." (Avenue Bhagwan was a road reserved exclusively for Him and the road service team.)

No one who was aware of Bhagwan's spending habits could believe the allegation that I stole millions of dollars from the commune reserve. Bhagwan had never allowed money to be put aside. In fact, He would always spend five times the amount to come in, even before it actually did. He once explained to me: "Remember, Seela, money has value only if it is in circulation. We should never have gold reserves. We should spend at least five times than we have, so that it circulates more. Only then is its real value used."

Bhagwan precisely calculated His gifts, and this in Indian rupees, so that they appeared very expensive. One day He handed me a beautiful pearl necklace and a watch that he wanted me to give to His mother and His uncle respectively. The pearls were old and valuable. The watch did not appear as expensive as the watches I had bought for Bhagwan on many occasions, but for an old Indian relative who valued gifts in Indian rupees, it was quite a gift. I cannot recall spending less than $20,000 on any of Bhagwan's watches. When He gave me these two pieces of jewellery, He instructed me: "Seela, these pearls are for my mother, and this watch is for my uncle . . . Tell my mother that the pearls are worth several hundred thousand rupees and the watch one hundred thousand rupees . . ."

"Do you really want me to tell them the prices?" I asked Him, even though I knew that His answer would be yes.

Bhagwan always wanted me to do everything exactly according to His instructions. These pearls were a gift from a European Sannyasin to Bhagwan. All donated jewellery and other exclusive items were brought directly to Him. He kept what interested Him, and the rest was distributed according to His wishes. He was very particular about this. He wanted everyone to know the value of His gifts. He even used them to promote or reduce the status of a person in the commune. Consequently, His gifts always became the central theme of gossip among the Sannyasins each time He distributed them. Bhagwan also had no reservations in asking me to reclaim His gift from a Sannyasin who had fallen out of His favour. Such situations were not pleasant for me, both from legal and moral standpoints. He and His organization were constantly threatened by such Sannyasins. One cannot trust demoted and disgruntled people.

These were the moments when I had to think about setting up organizations to protect Him from legal entanglements.

If I do not protect Him, His legal problems would quickly accumulate, I thought. The Rajneesh Jewellery Management Trust and the Rajneesh Car Collection Trust were two such cautionary measures. They were established to distance Bhagwan from these assets and to protect the valuables from claims against Him and the commune.

The wild accusations by Bhagwan, supported by His people, offered a convenient excuse to the US government to imprison me and to deport Bhagwan after they had discharged Him from investigative arrest. They confiscated everything they could lay their hands on and ensured that the commune was completely taken apart. After all they had to justify their own expenses for the extensive investigations that they had carried out for years to collect reasons for closing down the Rajneesh facilities in Oregon and around the world. They had waited for such an opportunity for years. My departure and Bhagwan's baseless accusations presented them with a much-needed break. After that, the destruction of the beautiful commune we had built was inevitable.

3
From the Black Forest to German prisons

Our six-week travel through Europe with the two journalists gave us time to become acquainted with our new reality. And this reality did not look bright. We realized we needed to do something ourselves if we wanted to survive.

We knew that if we worked together as a team, as we had done in Rajneeshpuram, our lives and future would become comfortable within a short period. We were a hard working, practical, and intelligent bunch of people with complementary capabilities. Making money to sustain ourselves couldn't be much of a problem, only if we tried. We came up with some ideas for businesses we could start. Also, we used the press as a means to multiply funds at our disposal by selling our story to interested journalists.

Finally we decided to open a hotel. We could put to good use the skills we had acquired in Rajneeshpuram to successfully run a hotel. We soon found a suitable location in the Black Forest. We chose this area for several reasons: Firstly, Germany was a member of the EC, which meant an opportunity to get a work permit for almost all of us. Secondly, Dipo and I were

Swiss nationals, and the Black Forest was not far for us. And, lastly, we loved the natural beauty of the Black Forest. We did not want to live in a big city. We wanted to work amidst serenity.

I soon signed a preliminary contract for the purchase of the hotel. It was easy to obtain loans since my popularity also gave people the wrong impression that I had somehow run off with $55 million. Most were ready to do business with me. The same day we sat together in the evening and talked about the possibility of moving in within a few days. Suddenly we heard several cars turn into the driveway of our guesthouse. Somebody stood up and looked out of the window. A bunch of policemen were running around to surround the house as in a raid. I laughed and said, "Maybe they have come to arrest us." I was just joking, but it turned out to be serious: they had really come to arrest me and two of my girlfriends because of an indictment for conspiring to murder Dr Devaraj. A day before this, the US government had filed an extradition request with the German authorities, apparently disregarding the immigration laws of Germany. But the German government had rejected this request to arrest and extradite me. So twenty-four hours later, the US government had filed a new extradition request under a new indictment. This time, they got lucky.

Four days before this, during negotiations for the purchase of the hotel, I had met a German lawyer and I had liked him. Just for fun, at that time, I had asked for his business card, saying, ". . . in case I am arrested, then I know whom I can call." I had never thought that this joke would soon turn into reality. As it turned out later, he was a gift from Existence.

Contrary to how I was being portrayed in the press,

I was not a criminal. I had done nothing that was illegal or prohibited. During the construction of Rajneeshpuram, I had followed the laws in an intelligent way and had applied them in accordance with the instructions of our lawyers. Criminal activities were not for me. So I felt I had nothing to fear.

During the interviews many journalists had asked, "Why don't you go to Switzerland? There, you're protected, because Switzerland does not extradite its own citizens. In addition, Switzerland is only a few miles away, just across the Rhine . . ." But, I never felt that I should protect myself from Bhagwan's outrageous accusations. I'd felt that any sensible person would be able to see how little truth there was in them.

So, in my view, I had no reason to fear anything. As it turned out, my views on justice and law were quite naive. I was very gullible and used to think that laws are there to protect the innocent. But, now that I am experienced, I believe that laws are there to protect criminals and the special interest of the powerful. They help politicians strengthen their positions and are a means to eliminate politically undesirable elements, as was demonstrated in my case.

In addition to the three of us, Bhagwan was also arrested. Our simultaneous arrests could have given enough exciting material for a good Hollywood thriller. It certainly provided immense excitement and sensation to the media and the FBI. That evening, my prison career began.

There was some confusion when the German police came to arrest me. They were reinforced by numerous FBI agents who, it seems, specialize in creating exciting situations. The first thing that the American policemen and FBI agents probably learn in their training is drama and theater. Each of their arrests has the intrinsic possibility to become a famous blockbuster or bestseller. And with me they had really hit the jackpot. Journalists from all over the world crept around me. All parties wanted to make sure their performance was good enough to secure the first prize for the best supporting role. These agents were experts in creating a spectacle.

The only concern I then had was: do prisons have clean bed linen and toilets? This was also the first question that I put to my lawyer on the phone. I knew I would certainly be exhausted after this drama and would need some sound sleep.

4
Contrast between German and American prison systems

It seemed as if I had left Rajneeshpuram only to end up in a German jail. It did not look like a flight to freedom. At that time nothing made any sense, but today I understand the significance of everything.

My period in the prison was possibly an opportunity for me to learn something about time and physical freedom. As a result of my unforgettable prison experience, I was able to become inwardly independent. I learned to survive. I developed the strength to deal with anything—known or unknown. Even though I was never a fearful individual to begin with, I learned to become even more fearless. I view my prison time as a final step towards becoming more conscious of my own peace and inner harmony. The prison was a logical extension of the education I had received from Bhagwan. It was like a monastic experience that, perhaps, He had cleverly arranged to complete my development.

Before I was actually locked into one, I had many assumptions about prisons, mainly derived from movies and television. But the reality was very different. It was a totally different world in there, with peculiar rules of engagement and behaviour. To suddenly live outside of Rajneeshpuram was already a culture shock for me. The prison worsened the jolt to an altogether different degree. Within a short time I had been dumped from one planet to another, and then, immediately afterwards, on yet another totally different planet.

They had their own language in there, and I'm not talking just about German. I had not only to learn German, but I also had to learn the language of giant locks and keys and of the opening and closing of metal doors. That was totally alien to me. Until then, I had not spent a single day of my life in a room with the door closed.

In Germany, there was considerable public interest about me, and I was treated with much respect. Although the wardens and guards were nervous about my presence, they were also interested in the publicity surrounding me. This curiosity made them friendlier. However, they kept their distance: they did not want my "corruption" to put them in a negative spotlight. Hence, caution was their watchword.

From the prison in Bühl, I was transported by police helicopter to Frankfurt. From there, I was to be taken to the United States. The one-hour journey to Frankfurt showed the attitude of the German police towards me.

The police officers flying with me had brought photos of me with themselves to take my autograph. During the flight they clicked more photos. They were very curious and took advantage of the opportunity to get to know me. They treated me like a public figure. They were not unduly concerned with either the accusations levied against me or with the nature of these accusations. Instead, they made jokes about the FBI.

It was a very friendly flight, even though I was a prisoner. Consequently, I could relax a bit before it all were to come to an end. I had no idea what awaited me in the US.

In general, the living conditions were pretty good in the German prisons I was taken to. Visitors were allowed to bring fresh fruits and flowers; lawyers' visits were without supervision. The inmates were not treated like dirt, and there was no paranoia. The jailors did not work overtime to humiliate the prisoners, as was the case in the US. Bed linen, towels, and public toilets were also very clean. All in all, there was a civilized order that did not humiliate the prisoners in German jails.

The Waldshut prison where I was first taken was expectedly mobbed and besieged by journalists from all over the world. In the first three days, the staff had difficulty in even taking me for a walk in fresh air, because hundreds of cameramen were always lurking around. The superintendent told me very politely in the presence of my lawyer how difficult it was for him to have me under his supervision. He did not want to risk a public scandal by treating either the press or me wrongly. From the window of his office, he showed me some of the journalists, their cameras ready, waiting for a glimpse of me. He was pleased that my lawyer and I were prepared to cooperate.

Although I consider my time in prison a learning experience, life in there was difficult, especially in the prisons of the United States where the manner of communication between jailors and inmates was very tense and stressful, and where instances of disrespect and provocations from both sides were a daily occurrence.

I was shuffled between five different prisons, one after the other, in the US. The most pleasant and comfortable prison for me was the one in Hood River. It was very small. A maximum of three or four prisoners could be accommodated in there, and I was pleased to not have to constantly see a guard or warden. It had a very personal atmosphere. Apart from me, there was just another inmate, in the neighboring cell. It was quiet, not loud and brutal like the facilities in Pleasanton or San Diego. Unfortunately, I was kept in this small prison for only one week.

Next, I was housed for a short time in The Dalles, Oregon. There I met a woman who was my fan. She worked as a guard there. She had taken the trouble to find out about my background and some of my habits and knew all about my love for taking a shower. So she had prepared a specially cleaned shower room for me with a mat on the floor so that I did not have to leave the shower with wet feet. She was very proud to be the one on duty during the time I was to be held captive there. On meeting me, she told me, "I have cleaned this shower just the way you like it. I read with great interest everything that was written about you . . . I think I know you. You're a good person. I am proud of what you have done at the Muddy Ranch, turning a patch of desert into a beautiful town. I hope you are not ill-treated here." She even bent down to put the bathing mat in front of my shower room. I was touched by her opinion, for it came directly from the heart. And this from an American jail guard!

In a similar way, a guardian angel was also sent to me at the unpleasant, high-security prison of Pleasanton, California. One of the female wardens there made my life much easier. Three days before I was transported there, she had a dream that she must protect me from any harm. She could not understand why she had had this dream, especially since she had not even known that I was to be moved to Pleasanton. She became a close friend of mine. For the sake of her security, I do not have any contact with her any more, but she was an angel who cared for me fearlessly. She took photos of me while I worked in prison and sent them to my parents to let them know that I was okay and that they should not fear for me. She even visited my parents in India during her vacation time to assure them personally that everything was fine. She knew that my parents were my main concern and that it caused me pain thinking that they would be concerned and worried about me. She was truly a gift from Existence to me.

Pleasanton was one of the prisons in which attempts were made to demoralize me. They wanted to break my spirit. During the first three months, they did not even allow me, under various pretexts, to see my adopted daughter, whom I loved very much. While I was in prison my family was taking care of her. I never wanted her life to be disturbed by my fate. They did not allow me to see any other family member either, which was very difficult for me. They even sent away visitors who had undertaken long journeys to see me. All my requests were immediately rejected without offering me any reasons.

There were also constant provocations by the jail wardens and prison counsellors. Two of them particularly distinguished themselves in this exercise. While one of them looked like a witch, the second was simply a bitter woman. In addition, the head of the prison was a bulldog of a man. All of them together constantly waited for a good reason to put me in the clink (prison cell for serving extra penalties). They tried everything to hurt me and break me down.

If Existence had not protected me well, I would have been exposed to many extremely dangerous situations. For instance, in Pleasanton, one day I was suddenly moved to a new cell. I was not given any reason for this sudden shift. In prisons reasons are never given unless ordered by court. One just does what one is ordered to do. I did not want to give the jailors any opportunity for further humiliation by asking them questions either. By shifting me, they clearly wanted to provoke me, so they could treat me brutally. Recognizing that, I simply obeyed their commands and crushed their ambitions with my silence.

In this new cell, my cellmate was a young, African-American girl. She had been sentenced to two twelve-year terms: reports alleged she'd seriously injured several people with razor blades. She was psychotic and belonged in a mental institution, not in a prison where she could harm others or herself.

I learned about her background much later, months after I first met her. I had been deliberately moved into her cell. This was one of the methods used to teach me a lesson. They wanted to see me hurt and broken. I accidentally found out about their intentions when I happened to be waiting outside the office of my counsellor to get some information from my lawyer one day. She was unaware that I was waiting outside; the door to the office was open. I overheard her conversing with a colleague about me. She, knowing that I now lived in the same cell as that dangerous girl, said laughingly, "Now we will see how many days Dorothy needs to cut Sheela into pieces . . ." I could not believe my ears. I first thought that I might have misunderstood what was being said, but it turned out that what I'd heard was correct. The two counsellors continued discussing the topic in detail until they saw me standing outside.

They shouted at me—"We have no time for you. In addition, you should not stand around. Go back to your cell!"—and closed the door on my face.

My cellmate lived happily with me for six months until she ran into trouble again and attacked someone. This was not exactly what they had hoped from her. She had improved so much in the six months with me that her psychiatrist once met me to find out how I had been treating her. He wanted to know if I had taught her a meditation technique, because she had not attacked anybody for three months. During that period, she had reported to her work regularly, and the quality of her work had improved as well. She was looking much happier than before.

I had just treated her with respect. I had dealt with her as with any normal living being, a normal person. Never before had anybody talked with her like that. This had an enormous impact on her. After a week she actually became my protector. She did not allow me to go to the laundry by myself. One day she said, "The laundry is no place for you, Jackie Kennedy. It is dangerous there." She called me Mrs Kennedy because I was a real lady for her. She treated me very respectfully. After six months, when she was back in trouble, I was locked in the clink with her. This was the usual procedure in prison. She insisted that I had nothing to do with her act of violence. In fact she bargained with the authorities for my release from the prison. In return she promised to tell them all about her crimes. She wanted me to notice how honestly she confessed her guilt. She wanted me to be proud of her. I was proud of her at the time, and I still am today.

I became quite popular among the prisoners. They showed

their respect for me in many ways. I was seen as a loyal person, and that means a lot in prison. Once, I heard that a person who had given false testimony against me was also serving a prison sentence somewhere else. He was not being treated well by his fellow inmates because his testimony against me was known and prisoners dislike "snitches." To be an informer or a "snitch" is considered contemptible in prisons. If you are found to be one, none of your fellow inmates will ever help or trust you. My prison-mates did not like Bhagwan as well, because they believed He had betrayed me.

Apart from my loyalty, my urine was also was very popular. I never took any drugs, and, as a result, whenever there was a urine test, the drug addicts in the prison would ask me for my urine, which they would then submit as their own for testing.

During mealtimes many inmates liked to join me. I had decided not to complain about anything while in the prison. I had decided to accept with gratitude everything that came my way. Most inmates were discontented with the food. Their complaint of course was well founded. But I had decided to enjoy my meals just as if I myself had chosen them. In the initial days, I ate would be alone at my table. But after some days my fellow inmates came up to my table and asked whether they could join me. Soon my table would always be overcrowded no matter where I sat down. We would eat laughing and joking.

One day, one of the inmates who often sat at my table told me that she had been eating the prison food for quite a few years and was always in trouble because she was constantly complaining about it. She had observed that I ate my meals as if they were delicious pizzas and burgers. She also found me very peaceful. She could not understand this aberration.

Therefore, she had come to see what I ate and why I ate it so happily. Why was I so happy? She asked me if I really loved the food. I told her, "I love myself. I want to keep my body healthy. If I complain about the food and take it without love, then it will not be good for me. It will turn into poison in my body. I am grateful that I get three meals a day. There are poor people who don't get anything to eat for days. If I lament, it only makes me bitter. Acceptance is the only intelligent response. I eat with love and care for myself. This keeps me healthy in here." The others saw and felt this too. They felt attracted to me and my eating habits.

In the same way I helped my fellow inmates in many situations. I supported them with legal correspondence; I helped them remove their facial hair using a thread. I had learned this technique while growing up in India. In Indian beauty parlours, this is a very popular technique to remove facial hair. In the prison we were not allowed to use any sharp instruments, such as tweezers, since they could be used as a weapon, or a tool for breaking out. So I would pull out a small thread from a piece of cloth for the purpose and patiently and gently remove facial hair using it. I was always ready to do such favours for my fellow inmates without expecting anything in return. They'd be very surprised by these little gestures.

Pleasanton was a mixed prison. It was easy to fall in love there. Everyone was hungry for warm feelings. Though the inmates were allowed to sit together and talk, and go for walks, and hold hands, sex was prohibited. But, inmates frequently indulged in some moments of sexual pleasure by having someone keep a watch. This sentry would raise an alarm if a guard was approaching. For many couples, I was a reliable sentry. One had confidence in me. People knew I was not a traitor.

As the chairman of the Rajneesh religion, I was authorized by Bhagwan to carry out birth, death, and wedding ceremonies. I put that authority to good use for conducting wedding ceremonies in jail, both between men and women and between lesbians. Once I also conducted a death ceremony for a woman whose husband had died in another prison. She had been unable to say even a final goodbye to him. These ceremonies helped to heal some hearts and give them love and peace. If it was in my power to bring together two lovers, I was always ready to help.

Then, in San Diego I ran into a kind counsellor. He could not understand why I had been arrested, or why I had been placed in the high-security wing. After meeting me the first time, he did not get the impression that I could be a violent individual, or that I posed or could pose a threat to anybody. Also my body language did not appear brutal or criminal to him. From more than sixteen years of professional experience in prisons, he claimed he could tell when he had a criminal in front of him. This man helped me find a task by which I could earn a few extra days to have my remaining penalty reduced.

In this counsellor, I saw a ray of hope to end my term of imprisonment prematurely. I was given the task to repaint an entire block of prison cells completely on my own, within a very short time. In the high-security wing one got very few opportunities to get a detention reduction through good deeds. This was an extraordinary opportunity for me. I ended up saving the prison a lot of money through my work, because I was a very careful painter and wasted very little paint.

Because of the many time-related rules and restrictions of the prison, I had to devise a way to do this work within the allotted time. I was largely dependent on the friendliness and willingness of the jailors. While some of them allowed me to leave my cell for several hours at night in order to work, others were not helpful at all. They were unwilling to risk anything and, thus, categorically did not allow anyone to leave their cells. Leaving me locked up was safer for them and meant less work. Despite everything, I managed to paint the whole cell block alone to my counsellor's and the prison director's satisfaction. As I had saved money for the prison, I also got thirty extra days credited. As a result I came out of prison before Christmas.

The director of the prison wanted no publicity because of me. I had to leave very inconspicuously. That suited me well too. While inside, I had only one desire: to get out of the prison and America as quickly as possible. That is why I was happy to comply with his request. Once again Existence protected me.

Later I heard that in the week in which the counsellor and the director had planned my release, the government of Oregon was working on new accusations against me. They were planning to prevent my impending release. Of course, they had no idea that I had earned thirty extra days, courtesy my painting expertise. The director had not informed a single government agency about my early release. Every prison director had the power to release a selected few inmates—who had earned a few extra days—before Christmas. As a result of this, I once more had the last word in the matters of Oregon. Their plan, to reconvict me with new charges before my release, was sabotaged. Their revenge and their desire for public attention continued, however. Afraid that I might establish a new commune or collect Bhagwan's people around me again, they came up with new indictments.

The nightmare was not over; the horrors of captivity had not yet completely ended. But at least I had escaped the clutches of Oregon.

I stayed for thirty-nine months in prison. Existence protected me throughout the whole ordeal. It gave me the good sense to avoid problems and hazards. It offered me an unclouded intuition, which guided me unerringly. In these thirty-nine months I learned a lot.

It was time to come out of prison, out of prisons both physical and mental. Even Existence saw no reason why I should continue to waste time inside. It wanted me to be ready for the next phase of my life, the life of a normal person living in the world outside and utilizing everything learned in the alien environment of the prison to make life better. Once again my Khidr asked me to leave and start something new.

5
My experiences with the US legal system

Apart from enduring the emotional turbulences that come with being imprisoned, there were many more things I had to concern myself with in order to maintain my inner balance. For instance, I had to cope with a total lack of communication with my former colleagues and friends. While in prison, I had no vehicle directly exchange ideas with the people who meant something to me. This complete separation from my friends almost stifled me.

During my entire career as head of the commune, I had always emphasized that good communication reduces the volume of work and increases its quality. Lack of communication is often the cause of failure, both in private life and in business world. Most relationships fall apart because people refuse to communicate or because they do not know how to communicate and express their feelings. This is also the cause of many diseases.

Since I'm aware of the importance of healthy communication, I have always encouraged people to raise their voices and speak without fear—freely, directly, and sincerely. In Rajneeshpuram, I often had long meetings with the department heads from all over the world. I would sit with them and listen to everything they had to say. I encouraged them to be easy-going and to deal with pain, anger, jealousy, and other negative feelings with a hearty sense of humour. Most of these meetings would be important and serious in nature, but I'd try to make them enjoyable for everyone.

This uninhibited sharing of thoughts would lead to new ideas, and a fresh energy in the work routine. It created an open, friendly, and spirited atmosphere, where both ideas and feelings were exchanged. This was one of the fundamental management changes that I brought to the institution. This was in stark contrast to the management style employed by my predecessor, Laxmi. I brought openness in our dealings with both the internal and the external worlds. The impact of this on the organization was noticeable. This openness helped me in my areas of weakness. I would derive strength from the ideas and feelings of others. This led to a better overall balance.

Open channels of communication were ever more important for me as my work and position were authoritarian. This position of authority given to me by Bhagwan automatically created awe, distance, and fear in other people. It was a great barrier, and I wanted to eliminate it. I wanted to remove the distance between my people and me. For this, communication at all levels was the only solution.

In the storm set off by Bhagwan with His daily new allegations, and due to the incredible interest of the press in me and the dramatic arrest, everything went out of balance. I, and all those who had left after me, were constantly subjected to hatred and rejection. The ship of our lives rocked from one side to the other, swept by the waves of false and ugly accusations and the negativity spread by Bhagwan and His followers.

In such a scenario, communication was our only anchor. But even it got lost in the mess following our arrests. Thereafter, I did not get any opportunity to speak directly with anyone. I could send messages only through my lawyers, which meant everything I said could be used against me. For the first time I understood the importance of weighing words before speaking them. The wise say: "Weigh your words before they come out of your mouth." In those days, for the first time in life, I understood the gravity of these words. I had to learn this important lesson in the midst of the crisis. Therefore, I often think and feel that Bhagwan "staged" all this only to further my growth and development.

As I mentioned previously, Existence had brought me in contact with a very conscientious lawyer when I was search for a hotel in Germany. He was a young man named Otmar whom I had instantly liked. I had found him honest. He had come to negotiate the purchase of the hotel on his client's behalf. Without deceiving his client, he gave me his honest opinion on the purchase we were negotiating. He did not want to be dishonest or misleading. During our talks, I managed to condense my contact with him. He gave me his business card as well as his private phone number. In the situation I was in, I could not tell when I might need a lawyer suddenly.

During my entire career in prison, Otmar approved to be a very valuable asset. He not only offered me his services as a lawyer, but also his shoulder to cry on in moments of sheer frustration. He had such a sensitive temperament that he would also shed a tear or two from time to time with me.

The rumour that I had stolen $55 million from the commune brought many greedy vultures to circle over me. Some of them were in the disguise of lawyers. It was difficult to recognize them for what they were at the time because I was in a hopeless situation. When I'd meet such vultures, I'd feel as if I had been chained and locked into a metal box and then thrown into the sea with no air to breathe. I'd try to come out of this box by imagining in my mind all kinds of ideas and illusions. The realization that I was being exploited in every way completely depressed me, and sometimes I'd see no way of coming out ever again from that nightmare. At such times, everything would seem pitch dark. In frustration, I'd even plan jailbreaks in my mind. These were dangerous thoughts, but then hopelessness does *not* encourage rational thinking. In a situation like this, the worst thoughts come to your mind. Fortunately, with Otmar around, I could talk with someone about all this madness.

The American lawyers, at least the one I met, were especially a dangerous breed. When I was in charge at Rajneeshpuram, I mainly had to deal with Sannyasin lawyers, which, though not always pleasant, was never as bad as dealing with lawyers outside. I am sure that my assistants—Homa, Vidya, and Savita—would have much more to tell about their terrible experiences with these vultures than I do. A few American lawyers and prosecutors made even Otmar come home weeping. Once he came back from a flight to the United States completely disheartened and unnerved. He had met a trial lawyer in Portland and had talked with him and the attorney general of the state about a plea bargain agreement.

In the American court system, this is a common approach to save time and costs. This method is also popular to wind up cases where there is little or no evidence. This is an exchange between two parties—the accused and the attorney general— similar to a game of poker. Both parties are aware of their good cards and bad cards. On the basis of these cards, an agreement is negotiated.

In my case, the bad cards in my hand were that I had no money to be represented in court by a good defender. The estimated cost for a trial, without any guarantee about the outcome, was an enormous sum of $2 million. Next, I had almost no chance of getting an objective grand jury, because I was very well known in Oregon, and the general population was against all Rajneeshees. There was considerable public interest in the case due to our prior conflicts with the culture and society of Oregon, and the public wanted to strike back at us. The politicians were of the opinion that it would be beneficial to destroy Bhagwan and me. Due to the international publicity that it had garnered, my case was very important to the public prosecutor and the attorney general. The justice department was under tremendous pressure from a public that wanted to see some action.

My good cards consisted of my positive attitude and my clear conscience, but unfortunately these were not good enough to make up for my bad cards. I was not guilty. I had committed no crimes. All allegations were based solely on hearsay and falsely gathered evidence as far as I was concerned. There were people, many of them foreign citizens living in Rajneeshpuram, who were to ready to testify against me as prosecutor's witnesses in order to secure their own freedom and stay in the US. They were accused of the same crimes I was accused of, so they were trying to buy their freedom by making false statements against me. It is important to understand that their sole motivation to become prosecutor's witnesses was to avoid being arrested. They were cowardly and dishonest.

The prosecution's major bad card was an overwhelming lack of evidence, despite the fact that the authorities had spent a fortune on the inquiries. Political careers were at stake as well. Their good cards were that the public was on their side. They had power and the financial resources to carry them through a court trial. They could easily find a grand jury that would willingly sentence me in absence of solid evidence.

Since I had no money, I had to make do with a public defender in Oregon. My chances looked very bleak. Otmar knew it. He met with this public defender in Portland. Otmar told me that he had to run out in the middle of this meeting in order to throw up. Not because he had salmonella poisoning, but because the contents of the meeting and the expected outcome had made him sick to the stomach. The Portland lawyer wanted to sell me to the attorney general. Otmar had never heard of such a thing during his entire career in Germany. In Germany one would have found this behaviour immoral or even interpretable as illegal. It was clear that the prosecutors and the public defender were sleeping under the same blanket. They had worked together during their whole lives. The public defendants alternated daily, and their loyalty dwindled in the direction of whatever was expedient for their career.

When Otmar told me about the tone and content of this meeting and how he had felt, I could understand why he looked as if a truck had run over him. He told me about the sentence the lawyer had wanted to negotiate for me: ten years of prison and a fine of one million dollars! Allegedly a good outcome according to the public defendant!

I was horrified. My first response was, "Is he crazy?" Otmar wept. He said, "Sheeli, you cannot accept this. It is not correct. I have seen some of the evidence. With this evidence, they cannot go to court . . . at least not if we were in Germany. They would have no chance." He wasn't saying this just to make me feel better. There was truth in it.

My first encounter with this lawyer was during my first night in jail in Portland after I had accepted my extradition. I had not tried to fight it. I wanted to solve the crazy situation as soon as possible.

In the middle of the night, around two o'clock, I was awakened. A lawyer wanted to speak to me. I could not believe it. I thought this must be some bad joke. I was full of suspicion and asked the jail warden, "Are you sure that a lawyer is here to see me? I do not think that I have a lawyer in Portland. My lawyer is in Germany . . ."

She assured me that there *was* a lawyer waiting for me in the visitors' room. I understood it as: there was someone in the visitors' room who claimed to be my lawyer.

He proved to be a lawyer all right. He told me he had worked for a while with Otmar to negotiate a settlement for me with the attorney general. He said he had seen earlier in the evening news that I had been brought to the Portland county jail. He had come to tell me that for him to represent me in the first hearing, I must immediately give him $38,000 as payment for the work he had already done on my behalf, and that I must pay him in advance for all further work! I was sure that this was an error since Otmar had told me nothing of this nature. He always used to discuss all the details with me.

Both his outrageous financial claim and my difficult situation made me very angry. I asked him about this supposedly open bill. He had never sent this bill to us but now wanted this sum of money just for reading all the articles about me. But no one had asked him to read all that! And what had the newspaper articles to do with my legal situation? I could not believe that this man had the impudence to see me in the middle of the night to tell me that he would represent me only if I immediately paid him $38,000. Even if I had $55 million, I would still have to make arrangements for such a large payment. I would not have carried that much cash with me. I told him to go. I told him that he could talk with a lawyer in Chicago who was also representing me and who was making all my payments. I thanked him for his visit and told him I did not need his representation. Then I called the warden and walked out.

The kind of situation I had been put in by the rumours about the $55 million was remarkable—everyone wanted to have a piece of it, but nobody was willing to examine the validity of the rumours. Of course not. The world was excited and scandalized to learn that I had stolen $55 million and wanted to put me in jail for it. But it had no objection in somehow snatching a part of it. I was appalled at this hypocrisy.

Coming back to that lawyer, never before had I seen such a crude behaviour in someone whose profession was to defend those people who did not have enough resources to hire a regular attorney. In my opinion, that lawyer was as a criminal. He robbed people who were caught in a hopeless state. Did he think for a moment how I felt, or what emotional turmoil I was going through? Did he even for a moment think how he would have felt in my situation if someone were to treat him this way? Only people with feelings can observe this. For me, he was not human. Strangely, next morning his partner showed up and apologized for his behaviour.

It was not easy. I had to be alert every moment. I would have preferred to bury my head in the sand like an ostrich and forget that I was in danger. But the school of life does not offer such luxuries. Awareness has to be the answer always.

A young man came to a Zen Master to learn about meditation. The Zen Master said, "Are you capable of waiting?"

The young man, of course, asked, "How long?"

The Zen Master said, "That is enough for me to reject you. To ask 'how long?' means you are not ready to wait. If you can simply wait without asking 'how long?' then you are capable of waiting."

The young man understood the point. He bowed down, remained with the Master.

One year passed, and not a single word was said to the disciple. And two years passed... and three years passed... "Now it is too much! Nothing has even been started, not a single lesson. How long can one wait?" Again the question became very prominent in his consciousness: "How long?"

He went to the Master and asked, "I have waited three years." The Master said, "So you have been counting? That simply shows you don't know how to wait. Counting? Counting days with the Master?

"In one sense, each moment is an eternity; in another sense, eternity is just a moment. You are unworthy! You will have to wait. You will have to learn how to wait. Be alert — from tomorrow the lessons will start."

And the lesson was very strange: the young man was sweeping the floor; the Master came from behind and hit him hard with his staff on his back. Shocked, the young man said, "Is this the beginning of meditation? After three years of waiting?" The Master said, "Yes – now be alert. I will hit you any moment, any time – be watchful, be alert, be on your guard." And it continued for months. His whole body would ache in the night, because in the day many times it would happen: the Master would suddenly jump from somewhere... he was very old but he was really a cat.

But, slowly, slowly, a strange awareness started arising in the young man. Just when the Master would be on the verge of hitting him, he would dodge – even from the back; although he was occupied in his work a subtle awareness remained there. It was bound to be so; he was suffering so much. Pain is a must for growth, suffering is absolutely necessary for growth. Unless you suffer you cannot be aware. Suffering brings awareness, and voluntary suffering brings tremendous awareness. Willingly he was suffering! He could have escaped; nobody was preventing him – it was his own choice. He had chosen the Master.

And now he started to understand why: "This is his teaching. This is how he is teaching meditation!" Now it dawned in his consciousness. He was immensely grateful.

The day the Master came from the back and, just before he was going to hit him, the young man jumped, dodged, and the stick of the Master fell on the ground, the young man was immensely happy. Something new had happened in his being. And the Master blessed him.

But from that day, things became even more difficult... the Master started hitting him while he was asleep. Now, this was too much. In the night, any time...! And the Master was very old; naturally, he could not sleep much, so whenever he felt awake he would go and hit the young man. But now the young man knew: "I may not understand the process of it, but the Master's hitting in the day has been of such immense benediction, has caused such a transformation, that I accept this too – without any questions." He didn't ask, "This is absurd, this is ridiculous. It is okay that you hit me in the day – I can at least protect myself, run away, escape, dodge – but what can I do when I am asleep?" He didn't say it.

And the Master said, "This is a good sign. For the first time you are learning trust – you have not asked the question."

And after two, three months of being hit in the night, the whole day his body would ache. In the day he was able now to protect himself... but one day in the night it happened!

The Master entered the room and he opened his eyes. He said, "Wait! I am awake."

And it happened more and more. It became impossible to hit him. Immediately the Master entered into the room he opened his eyes – as if he was not asleep at all. That was not so: he was fast asleep, but a part of his being was released from the physical sleep, the tip of the iceberg, just a small part, but it went on like a lit candle inside – watching, waiting.

The Master was very happy. The next day in the morning, the Master was sitting underneath a tree reading some old sutras, some old scripture. Suddenly – the young man was sweeping the garden – an idea arose in him: "This old man has been hitting me for almost one year, day in, day out – how will it be if I try once to hit him? It will be worth seeing how HE reacts."

And the Master closed his sutras and said, "You fool! I am an old man! Don't have such ideas."

(From "An Alive Buddhafield," in *Osho: The Fish in the Sea is Not Thirsty*)

I had many shocking experiences in the US courts as well. Once I encountered a federal judge who was counting his votes during my hearing. When he saw many future voters sitting in the courtroom on whose votes he was dependent in the next elections, he immediately began his campaign at my cost. His task was really only to decide my settlement agreement. It was a simple hearing to ensure the consent of all parties on this agreement. His court had only to verify this and then sign and stamp the papers. But he used this opportunity to give me a sermon in order to obtain the approval of his voter audience. In my view, he acted very unprofessionally. Corruption really runs through the entire system.

To help me wade through all this corruption, I had thankfully found a good team of lawyers—Otmar, Steve, and Marvin. They worked as a team for me. Steven House, a very good lawyer from Portland, took over my defence. He represented my case well and took care of my interests. He was always available when I needed his help. Marvin, whom I had known for many years, used to practice tax and business law in Chicago. He was a friend of my family, especially of my brother Bipin. Over the years I had consulted Marvin for legal advice a number of times. He had even been involved in drawing up the first contracts for the purchase of land for the construction of the commune in Oregon. Marvin was a funny man with a typical Jewish sense of humour, which would bring me some much-needed relief during stressful times. He helped me find lawyers in America and coordinated their work so that they could represent me. With Savita's help, he also worked out the fees of all the lawyers. This team of lawyers was a gift of Existence to me. With their help, I was able to negotiate a good settlement agreement.

I accepted a negotiated sentence of four-and-a-half years imprisonment for all counts of indictment against me. I agreed to plead guilty to a narrowed set of violations involving immigration fraud and interception of telephone communication. For all other indictment points, I pleaded "not guilty," according to the precedent "Alford against North Carolina". It is a plea under which a defendant may choose to plead guilty, not because he or she admits to the crime, but because the prosecutor has sufficient evidence to place a charge and to obtain conviction in court. It's an "I'm guilty but I didn't do it" plea.

In my understanding, a settlement agreement is approved by the courts only if the court believes that the accused is truly innocent on the counts for which a "not guilty" plea is entered. In my case and in the case of two of my co-accused, the courts had happily agreed to this agreement. This agreement is a confirmation of my view of my innocence. If I was guilty of the charges, the prosecutor would never have accepted the agreement both for legal and juridical reasons.

These preposterous charges could have never been proven in a way four-and-a-half years of imprisonment could be awarded. But under the given circumstances, to avoid a long and expensive trial, I had to agree to a prison term. Also, even the attorney general, after extensive inquiries, came to a conclusion that there never were in Rajneeshpuram $55 million. Everything they had seized in the form of watches and jewellery was not mine; it belonged to Bhagwan and the trust I had set up for these items. The money for His release came from His people, not from me.

My dealings with the law, the lawyers, the attorney general, the courts, and jails have almost made me an amateur expert in matters of US law. My advice to everyone would be to stay as far away as possible from all this vileness.

6
The nightmare continues

After my release from San Diego, I went to Germany to begin a new life. In Europe I still had some contacts. I had many ideas but no clear direction. I had no clue of what life was going to give me next. I was completely groping in the dark. Some friends, who had helped me survive the horrors of detention, had gone their own ways. Meanwhile, Dipo, my Swiss husband, had passed away while I was still in the US prison. I was alone, completely alone.

Of course I was faced with the same financial realities with which every human being has to cope. Deep down I felt completely lost. I did not know where to turn or what to do. All I knew somewhere deep in my heart was that at the right time, at the right place, the right opportunity would turn up. I decided to start my life anew in the southwestern part of Germany where we had set up a hotel before my arrest and which was also near the village where Otmar, my attorney, lived.

I did not have many talents. My skills were mainly limited to managing a large commune and to pass on Bhagwan's orders.

I did not have the slightest experience of how to function in the outside world.

Then suddenly, one day, my entry into Germany was denied. I had driven across the border to go shopping in Switzerland. I would do this regularly while living in Germany. On the return trip, like always, I had to go through passport control. But my re-entry was denied without giving me any reasons. At that moment I again felt as if the rug had been pulled out from under my feet. No reasons, no explanations were given. I could only conclude that it was a political decision. This was a hard blow for me, because, all of a sudden, I had been separated from the man I was in love with and the man who could guide me.

Otmar and I had fallen in love while I was in prison in Germany. He would visit me in the prison and shower me with love and comfort. His daily love letters and beautiful flowers and fruits were a sweet, cooling balm for my wounded heart. The heat of the love between us had not cooled even though I had rejected him when I was in prison. In prison, one is in need. I could not separate myself from this feeling of need. So I could not be sure whether I loved him because I needed him or because I truly loved him. Also, I was not prepared to commit myself to someone when I was so unsure of the future. So, during the time in prison I behaved very frigidly with him in this regard. I am sure that I hurt him with that.

But, after my release, being with him again had heated up the passion between us. We had spent wonderful moments together, despite certain practical and emotional problems. I was free, available to him, but he was not free. During my time in prison he had met another woman. He now lived with her. She was slightly handicapped by a stroke. He was full of guilt since his heart was split between love and responsibility. It nearly tore him apart. He was torn between his love for me and his feelings of responsibility for this woman. He had a law firm, a son, and his girlfriend. So he closed the doors of his heart. Love was not his priority. The guilt won, and he turned his back on me. He was not prepared to drop his safe existence to lead an insecure life full of complications with me. By now I had enough experience of how it felt to be shunned by everyone.

The harsh reality had once again shown its true face to me. I felt lost. Without any clear direction, it was very difficult for me to go on. The only thing that was still functioning was my sense of the practical, which has so often proven to be a great gift. Once again it came to my aid. No long-term solutions emerged from it, but it carried me from one moment to the next. The strong faith in my heart that it would lead me to the right place at the right time helped me to lift my head high and follow the orders of my pragmatic mind.

Three things made life difficult, joyless, and uncomfortable: a broken love affair, the fear of losing my freedom again, and having very little money. I dreamed of finding a solution to all my problems. I dreamed of living the rest of my life happily with my German lover. I waited endlessly to hear his voice on the phone or for him to come to my rescue. In vain I imagined every day that we would get back together and will always and forever remain together. This only gave me additional problems. I was depressed, sick, sad, hurt, and wounded. Sometimes I waited for hours next to the telephone in the hope that it would ring and bring a new, hopeful message for my heart. The sweet, charming voice of my beloved would cheer me up. These were days full of disappointments, the nights full of loneliness. Surprisingly there was no bitterness and no complaints in me, only sadness. There was nothing left for me than to accept everything and to wait. I often remembered Buddha's words: "This too shall pass." One thing I learned from all this: everything does pass. Even the time in prison, which had seemed so slow, had finally passed.

This interplay between fate and a sense of the practical resulted in my going to Portugal.

Portugal is a poor country. I was also poor. So I immediately felt at home there. It was easy to create a small home for me here. The people in Portugal are simple. Their life revolves around daily necessities. Their existential and luxurious needs are those similar to a Third World Country. I had made a good choice to go there in my situation. The basic food was cheap. Life in Portugal was not exciting. I could spend some time there, until another direction for my life emerged. I isolated myself. It was easy, and it was necessary. I felt safe in this isolation. I felt healthy in the mood I was in. From time to time curious people tried to contact me. But the basic problem—that I did not understand their language—protected me from these visitors.

My home in Portugal was a small hut surrounded by a small forest of eucalyptus trees. There I lived with a young Japanese writer. Her name was Mayumi. She was a very sensitive woman who had come to Portugal because of a health crisis. She was ill with cancer and had left Japan and her familiar surroundings to write a little. She wanted to better understand herself and her disease. We had come to know each other at a village festival. I offered to share my little hut with her. She brought pleasure into my lonely life. In addition, my spending became less because she shared rent and meals with me. We lived very harmoniously with each other and had a lot of joy. Since we cooked for each other, food also became interesting again. After she moved into my hut, my life became happier. I no longer suffered from love-grief. I found new energy and did not wait day and night any longer for a call from Otmar. Mayumi was a very sincere friend. Her gift to me is the design of the logo for my institution, which reminds me fondly of her every time I see it.

Previously, I simply ate in order to survive. My food money was very limited. During my stay in Portugal, I could spend only fifty German marks per month. Even this money was borrowed from friends. By myself, I ate only a couple of eggs and some bread in a day, and drank wine. Wine was very inexpensive in Portugal. Sometimes I allowed myself a piece of cheese too. I just took life as it offered itself to me. I did not claim anything. I did not complain. I was just grateful to be free again.

Approximately eight months later in this dark time, a sudden event again led to a change. Apparently, Otmar had been trying to reach me for a week. I called him back when I finally received his message. He had important news for me. Two journalists from Oregon were in contact with him. They'd warned him that I would be faced with further legal complications. The next elections were coming up and the local politicians in Oregon were looking for opportunities for media coverage. My name was still good for publicity. Politicians hungry for media attention could benefit enormously from me. I still played an important role in the local politics of Oregon. For that reason, further false accusations were going to be raised against me.

These two journalists wanted to inform me so that I could go into hiding. Ironically, in the past, they had written scandalous, sensationally made-up articles about me in which I had been painted as a terrible monster and a terrorist. Now they were suddenly warning me of the risks I was going to face. The methodology used by the US government shocked me. It showed a clear disrespect of the Constitution and the law. But I was even more astonished about the warning from these two journalists. If they were really convinced by the horror stories that they had written about me, why did they want to protect me? Why protect a monster, a terrorist? To any intelligent person, it was obvious that the accusations against me were not credible, but flimsy and politically motivated. They were far removed from reality.

This news from Otmar caused many concerns. I became worried. My reality seemed to me like an ugly pimple, which seemed ready to burst. I was no longer naive. I had had my share of experiences with the courts and the judicial authorities in the US. I had to move on now. I had to move on to safeguard my freedom. I did not want to repeat my mistakes. Once again the question arose—where should I go? Where would I be safe? I quickly went through all the possibilities. My lawyer Otmar was not sure if Switzerland would provide protection to me, although through my marriage to Dipo I was a Swiss citizen. Bhagwan in His ugly anger had tried to raise doubt about this and had accused me of bigamy. Though it's true I had another lover, Jay, at the time, I was never married to him officially. Bhagwan had thought that my controversial lifestyle would influence the courts to give in to prejudices and go for a political decision against me. Fortunately the Swiss courts acted wisely and validated my marriage.

It was a desperate situation, and I really had to act. I could not ignore the communication of the two journalists from Oregon. I had to protect myself from all possible consequences.

Until then, I had always said yes to everything that had happened. So now once again I did not want to say no. For a moment I closed my eyes and looked into my heart. The answer came: I must leave Portugal immediately. I must go to Switzerland where I could at least hope to be protected from the legal attack by the US government.

7
Onwards to Switzerland

My legal situation now forced me to leave Portugal. But I did not want to go away without explaining my complicated legal life to Mayumi. She had earned my confidence through her friendship. She was a part of my life. She had given comfort to me when I needed it. She deserved to know everything about me. I tried to explain it to her, but she loved me so much that she did not need any explanation. She simply wanted to assist me in this crisis without much fuss or acknowledgement. She trusted me. She had lived with me for six months. We had spent a very valuable time together. She had learned a lot from me and I from her. Mayumi knew that I did not have much money. She felt that money would ease my journey into the unknown. So she emptied her wallet and gave me its entire contents. It was not much, but was enough to help me for then. All she asked of me was for me to send her a message about how I was getting along as soon as I could.

She was not a Sannyasin. She was not in search of enlightenment, and, therefore, the greed for enlightenment did not stand in the way of her experience with me.

Her simple affection touched me deeply. I kissed her farewell on the forehead. She is one of those very rare friends that I can count on in times of need even today. She visited me in Switzerland in 2007. Her dream of becoming a novelist was fulfilled last year with the publication of her first book. We still correspond with each other.

When I left Portugal, I just knew that I wanted to return to Switzerland. I had a strong feeling that I'd be safe there. I decided to go to Basel, because there I could still be in the vicinity of my beloved Otmar. He'd just be a few kilometers on the other side of the border in Germany. I hoped that this would heal my broken heart.

8
A new beginning in Switzerland

Life after my release from prison was a major legal chess game. I always tried to be one step ahead of my opponents. The return ticket to Switzerland, which I had with me when I went to Portugal, was one such additional move.

After my sudden departure from Portugal, I arrived late in the evening in Basel, full of expectations to meet my beloved Otmar. But these expectations turned into disappointment in less than a moment. Hoping to find Otmar, I ran up and down the station. My heart was hurting and my head was heavy from a maelstrom of emotions. My body was exhausted from the twenty-four-hour trip. I had been stopped at every border check point. The fear of the authorities was overpowering.

While waiting for Otmar at the station, I saw a Sannyasin standing in the middle of a group of people. She was a well-known therapist from Rajneeshpuram. I have forgotten her name. She was standing there with some other young people. When her eyes met mine, she took a second look to make sure it was me. Then she started to smile, but suddenly her face froze, as if she had done something illegal. She wanted to wave at me, but it was as if someone held back her hand. Difficult for her, and sad for me to watch.

This event was healthy for me because it deflected my attention for a short while from my plight, my problems, and my fatigue.

In this moment I saw and felt that she was much more of a prisoner than I was. Her smile did not belong to her. She did not have the freedom to do what she wanted to do. She could not be herself. She could not freely express her own feelings. She was not the master of her own self.

This realization immediately lifted my mood. I felt I was in a much better position than that therapist. My smile still belonged to me. I had not allowed it to be controlled by anything or anybody, not even by my thirty-nine months in prison. I laughed. It was ironic and surprising that she—a prisoner herself—helped other people through group therapy to escape their prisons. What a contradiction!

To watch this Sannyasin in her dilemma helped me clear up my thoughts. I prepared myself to take the next step in Switzerland. I had the necessary confidence in myself. I was my own master. I did not have to behave and feel according to someone else's whims. I could do what I wanted.

This trip had begun with the disappointment from a lover. Now I did not want love or a lover to be my weakness. Also, it was not good to ignore the practical aspects of life. First I had to find a place where I could stay and get some rest. I had learned one thing: no one else cares about me. I could not count on anybody, not even on my lover. I let my focus shift from my heart to my mind. My mind led me to a hotel opposite the railway station.

There I got a small but clean and comfortable room with a shower at a price that I could afford. Normally it is very difficult to find a reasonable accommodation in the middle of Basel. But to my surprise this was something very suitable for me. This was clearly a miracle, an example that Existence always looks after me.

I ordered my mind to be still, because calm mental state is always most important. The next morning I had a lot to do. I had to look for an accommodation where I could spend the coming nights. Above all, I immediately needed a job in order to survive. I had learned survival in prison. I benefitted then, and continue to benefit, from each and every experience my ordeal had pushed me through. But first I wanted to rest. I learned to take only one step at a time. I learned to live in the present. I did not worry about the coming future.

The next morning I immediately started. It was important to be careful. I had very little money left. I could not afford much with it. I had to spend each penny economically and carefully. I could not afford to be sloppy or careless.

I visited various job agencies to seek employment. For now this was the most important thing. People found me strange. I obviously was a foreigner. I spoke neither Swiss German nor German. I was looking for physical work, but had the manners of a manager. This did not make sense to the people I met.

But Existence once again sent me a guardian angel: a young woman named Aline who served coffee and croissants to me at an employment agency's office. She had an open ear for me and had liked me at first sight. She helped me with the necessary things to begin my life with in Switzerland. She told me about the basic social, economic, and legal considerations necessary to live in the country. She took care of the crucial documents I required. We became good friends. Even today we have a very special relationship with each other. She arranged the first three jobs for me in the country.

My first job was to walk Aline's grandparents' dog for an hour daily. For this I got ten Swiss francs per day. This was enough to feed me for one day. Through this I also learned the extent of loyalty an animal can show. Unfortunately this quality is very rare in humans. Rajneesh Sannyasins can particularly learn a lot about loyalty from these wonderful creatures.

My job of walking the dog turned into work-with-accommodation. I got promoted. Now I was no longer occupied only with walking the dog, but was also a domestic servant. This activity gave me a certain degree of legal security, because my host was one of the most famous lawyers in Basel. I talked openly to him about my legal problems. His advice reassured me and calmed me. He felt that there was no risk of extradition for me because I was legally a Swiss national. Switzerland does not extradite its own citizens. The only danger would be if I travelled outside the country. He strongly advised me not to go to Germany or France, not even for a mug of beer or a cup of coffee.

I also worried about the possibility that the US government might attempt to kidnap me. But he reassured me here too. Although he admitted that he knew of such incidents, he reassured me, explaining that abduction from Switzerland would be much more difficult than for instance from Germany since, unlike Germany, no American military was stationed in Switzerland. He also assured me that he would defend me until the end of his life if something like this were to happen. This assurance gave me a feeling that I was in the right place. Living in his house, I felt very safe.

I said yes to everything. I accepted what life offered me in love: a palace, a prison, or a hut. I had become the Yes.

I worked for about eight months for this old couple. My life during this time was peaceful. I had steady income. There was good food. I could sleep well. The domestic work improved my physical condition. I was again more in my body and got to know it better. The beautiful dog, his name was Barry, made my heart flower. He became my friend. Barry's friendship made me forget my love sickness. There was a loving understanding between us. Whenever he wanted to go out, he would fetch my coat from the cloakroom and come to me. I was so dazzled by his innocence and purity that I would take him outside even in the middle of the night or even when it would be freezing outside. He took care of me, and I took care of him.

Barry was cute. Whenever I walked him, he was always very excited. He would often run to the middle of the road and roll around. All the cars would have to stop, and I would have to beg him to stand up again and get out of the traffic's way. But the more I begged, the more he enjoyed rolling around on the road. The people on the street would curse at Barry and me, but I was never offended by this. It was so beautiful to watch this noble animal in his joy.

Soon, a certain degree of normality returned to my life. For one, I earned enough money to gradually pay back the debts I had accumulated since my release from prison. Then I felt my strength and confidence coming back. Now I was no longer busy twenty-four hours a day worrying about my legal problems. I gained much strength from the simple work. It all felt so healthy I even hoped my heart would heal.

Just when this new direction in my life had started to stabilize and as I was getting used to the daily routine, something happened that threw me off track again and forced me to start things anew. The two old people with whom I lived and for whom I worked were both already way into their eighties. They were very rich and very forgetful. The woman wore a valuable diamond ring, which she would often forget at the washbasin or in the kitchen or in the dining room. One evening it happened again. She left her ring somewhere.

It was my day off. I had gone out and had come back late in the evening. The old lady woke me up and asked me to immediately come into the office of her husband to discuss something. I was taken aback by the formality of her tone. My heart sank. Is it the Americans again? Will I be extradited?

As it transpired, these fears were unwarranted. I was only accused of stealing the old lady's diamond ring. The problem was of a different kind, but it could have its own legal consequences. Fortunately, during my daily housework I had had enough opportunity to observe the old lady's habits. Therefore I was instantly sure that the ring was only misplaced. I reconstructed in my mind the events of the previous evening and took only some seconds to find the ring. The old couple apologized profusely to me for the unjustified accusation. I accepted their apologies wholeheartedly, but didn't fail to notice a serious hazard in this incident. Something like this might happen again with me. One could not rely on the memory of the couple.

I decided to quit the job. I analyzed my feelings and realized that it made me happy to take care of old people. When I took care of the elderly, I felt closer and deeply connected to my beloved old parents who lived alone in India. Taking care of people has always been my vocation. When I was with my parents, I took care of them. When I was with Bhagwan, I took care of Him and His Sannyasins. And my first job had been about this as well. It became very clear to me that I should find a job related to nursing and giving care.

So, with the help of a newly acquired young friend, Urs Sager, I founded a private home for old people. I had met Urs while living in Basel. He was a friend of Aline. Urs and Aline had studied together and Aline had introduced me to him. Urs often accompanied Barry and me on our walks. He was a young man with little life experience. He had a hunch back and had lived with his parents until the age of thirty-five. When I'd met him the first time, he had just started living alone.

I was alone, and he was alone, so we became good friends soon.

Once, while I was still working with the old couple, I became sick and had high fever. I did not want to be a burden on the old couple with my illness, but I needed somebody to care for me. I was in a really bad state. I called Urs at his workplace and asked him if I could stay in his apartment for a few days until I was better and ready to go back to work. He immediately came over, took me to the doctor, and then to his apartment. For a week he lovingly nursed me. This care created familiarity and closeness between us.

One day I had a desire for sex. I asked him if he wanted to go to bed with me. He was shocked. Nobody had ever asked him for sex so directly and without making a fuss about it. He had never encountered such a direct expression of the fundamental need that sex is. He only knew that sexuality was something to be hidden.

I brought adventure into his life. I showed him contentment and honesty. He realized that many of his attitudes and views about life and its values were wrong.

I became a friend in whom he could confide in his innermost feelings and fears. Throughout his life he had felt he was an unwanted child. He felt inferior to his brother. His father yelled at him, and his mother dominated him. His brother had married and had bought a flat for himself; his parents always asked his brother for advice and counsel.

I know both Urs and his brother well. They were different. They could not be compared. They each had their own virtues and vices. Urs had one of those innocent, simple hearts that are hard to come by. He was not a great intellectual. The world anyway does not need more confusion through great intellectuals like Bhagwan.

His simple heart made me ask him if he would like to live and build a project with me. Being Swiss-born, he had no problem with the Swiss German language as I did, and to start something new in Switzerland it was necessary to speak Swiss German. He took care of all business conversations until I myself had learned a little German. I told him how critical his help through his language was to the project.

He showed courage. For the first time in his life he took some risk by becoming my partner despite knowing about my past. I was not an average person with an ordinary background. I had a whole history of sensations and scandals behind me. Any contact with me could be dangerous for anybody. Despite all this Urs showed trust in me.

Our home for old people was like a new school of life for me. I again got the opportunity to put Bhagwan's teachings into practice in everyday life. This new project required a lot of patience, attention, and thought. One had to be ready to help at any moment.

My empty life was immediately filled again. I had no time to brood over my past or to worry about the future. I was forced to be in the present, in the here and now. I did not have to pretend to meditate in order to be in the moment.

Life in a community is, according to Bhagwan, the only answer to the now widespread loneliness of man. That's why He had founded communes all over the world. But I had not consciously planned to establish a commune. It happened simply because I had internalized Bhagwan's teachings and had unknowingly let myself be led by them. My house soon became a living, breathing, thriving community similar to Rajneeshpuram.

Not before long, my home was filled with old people. And within a very short period of time, it became known for its quality and care. The doctors of my patients were surprised by how much one could do with mere loving care.

This success once again attracted the attention of the press towards me. Journalists came to write articles about my work with the old people. I used the opportunity to make them familiar with the problems of the old and disabled. Elderly need sympathy and love. It is important to understand that age is not a disease. The aging process is not ugly. However, isolation can make old age miserable.

I think that we, the young and the healthy, are a much bigger problem. We have lost interest in loving and caring for others. We are only busy in ourselves, in satiating the needs of our small minds. We need to become generous in our hearts. We need to open up to other people. We can do much for them, only if we keep our egos aside and try to understand the difficulties that these people face.

Unfortunately, when the journalists realized whom they were dealing with, they were a lot more interested in me than in the old people. They could not ignore me. And I—who had learned public relation tactics from Bhagwan—welcomed their attention. I used their interest in me to spread awareness about the cause I was working for.

One article followed another and soon the media gathered around me again. Through these publications I came into contact with many people. Among these was also the owner of the house in which I now live. For a long time he had been unable to rent or sell his expensive building which was located in a small Swiss village. Through me he saw a chance to put the property to good use and make a profit too. This arrangement suited me well, and I agreed to buy the property for the expansion of my work. He undertook the necessary construction work to adapt the house to the needs of old people. He needed me and I could use his house. All went well.

My home, where old and disabled people conveniently live together in a community and feel totally at home, is a model for the future. The needy in my home are fully integrated into the daily life. This integration is our answer to the problem of isolation. The whole house is free and open. We live together like a family. The residents don't have to subject themselves to the institutionalized lifestyle of nursing homes. In our house, nobody feels lonely or isolated. Everyone is surrounded by warmth and care.

Our house is an alternative to European retirement homes. The usual homes for the elderly are outdated in their concept. They provide good care but only in certain areas. In them, though the body is cared for well, the heart and the emotions are ignored. The time, the money, and above all the talent to do this are not exactly available in abundance.

Small groups of people of all ages living together like one big family—this is the answer to the problem of isolation that afflicts modern man. The lifestyle of a small nuclear family is not suitable in my opinion. It only contributes to the solitude of the heart. It draws one into a black hole of loneliness. Depressions become a daily problem. Houses like ours offer a warm, loving atmosphere.

While working with the elderly, I got had an opportunity to think of my own aging. The thought of spending my last days in a traditional nursing home frankly frightens me. I do not want to live in a public or private institution. With the care that is offered there, there is a lot of coldness. I would be lost without the warmth of a heart, without the love of fellow human beings. Such a situation would not be acceptable to me. I would want to retire only in a home like the one I have created.

Through a simple, basic concept, it is possible to help one another. Love and compassion must become the leading forces of our lives. I am sure that Existence will keep holding my hand and help me move forward.

Meanwhile, my life has meaning again, and my job is at its centre. My heart does not hurt anymore because of Otmar and my separation from him. I see him from time to time or sometimes I ring him up. I hear news about him through his mother, who has become a mother and a good friend of mine as well. My day is filled with work, which keeps me away from all the banalities of the outside world. I feel contented. I have come closer to my nature. I've become more and more aware of my needs and demands. My family supports me and my work. They have always done so. They have supported me unconditionally, even when the whole world had rejected me. Now my peaceful days have brought rest into their lives, and they no longer have to constantly worry about me and my fate. I don't have sleepless nights anymore because of the American judicial authorities. I know that Existence will take care of me no matter what situation I am in. It will give me enough strength to work through everything I face. Until now it has always been like this, and I know that it will continue to be like this. By and large I feel good. Sometimes even very good.

In the chapters that follow I'll go back to the beginning when I first met Bhagwan. I will describe how I became His private secretary, and how I moved the commune from Poona to Oregon. I have already recounted the events that led to my resignation from my position as the operating head of the commune in Rajneeshpuram and my odyssey through German and US prisons facing outrageously false accusations.

Let me now tell you how it all started.

TWO

9
How it all began

My life has always been full of events beyond my control. Often, things have happened in my life without my being aware of the reasons behind them. But today when I look back, it is clear that everything that has happened to me so far in life has happened exactly as it should have been.

My wise father is responsible for the fact that I came into contact with Bhagwan when I was just a young girl. At that time, Bhagwan would occasionally give lectures in my hometown. My father would always invite people like Bhagwan to our home. For him it was very important that we, his children, come in contact with high achievers from every field and learn to develop an open mind and a broad perspective in life from the experience. This was part of our education process. He wanted us to have choices and to be capable of finding our own values. He wanted us to have the freedom to do what we felt was best for us. Therefore he insisted on an all-inclusive education, a part of which was meeting leaders and thinkers from all walks of life. My father wanted to give us a wealth of knowledge that could guide us throughout our lives.

My father grew up in a small village in a province in Gujarat, India. When he was only three months old, his mother passed away. He was forced to leave his home when he was only seventeen over a dispute with his father: he did not want to accept an arranged marriage at that early an age to an even younger girl. This turned out to be a great blessing in disguise. Guided by a wise uncle, he joined Mahatma Gandhi's Sabarmati Ashram in Ahmedabad in mid-1920s. There he was noticed for his hard work and dedication by Sri Kakasaheb Kalelkar, a leading author, educator, and a member of Mahatmaji's inner circle. Sri Kakasaheb took him under his wing and mentored him. As Sri Kakasaheb's secretary, he received an extensive education in languages, literature, religion, and philosophy. During the ten years he spent in the Gandhi Ashram, he was in direct contact with Mahatmaji and would even sit in as his appointment-secretary during his meetings with national and international leaders. Later, he also spent several years in British jails as a political prisoner and freedom fighter. In recognition of his contribution in securing India's freedom, he received a prestigious award in 1978 from Prime Minister Indira Gandhi.

My parents have played a very special role in my life. They have enriched it in many ways through their love, guidance, and encouragement. I have a very beautiful connection with them. I am sure that my brothers and sisters also feel exactly the same about them.

Bhagwan had an unconventional take on the relationship between parents and children: "Remember, Seela, everyone should be able to choose their parents. The process of birth takes this choice away. The parents begin to possess their children. They push them around. The children lose their freedom. Some children resist . . . . justifiably.

"In our commune people will live in a changing family. The children will belong to the commune. They will belong to everybody, not just to one pair of parents. They will have their freedom . . . freedom of choice. It is important to understand that the process of birth is necessary for our existence. One should be grateful to one's parents for giving them birth and for the protection they provide. But there comes a time in life when one should find the parents of one's choice and when the parents should find children of their choice after their natural children have grown up. It is a problem in our society that such a choice is not supported.

"In our commune it will be possible. The commune will take care of the children. The children will not be bound to their natural parents. The parents will not hold on to their children just because they need someone to take care of them when they get old . . . In our commune old age will not be seen as ugly, but as something full of dignity . . . The elderly will be the teachers, they will be the source of the wisdom of life, they will teach love, they will show how to age beautifully and gracefully, they will teach how to die gracefully and with joy. The commune will take care of them when they can no longer take care of themselves . . . they will not be isolated and lonely . . . There will be no children just because one wants to use them for oneself. This problem will be eradicated. Then children will be grateful both for their birth as well as for the freedom to choose. Then parents and children will be able to choose each other . . ."

I am lucky. My parents for me are both—the parents

whom I have chosen as well as those who brought me into this world. My father was an intellectual with a warm heart, and my mother was just pure heart. She was a woman with a lot of practical sense. She was the force that always stood behind my father, and my father was her constant strength. They loved each other, and I loved them both.

I first met Bhagwan when He visited our home on my father's invitation. It was a profoundly enriching meeting. Ever since that fateful day nothing has been the same in my life. Bhagwan touched me somewhere deep inside. I did not understand much of what He said. But I could not erase Him from my memory. He remained present in me until we met again.

During those years I was living in the United States. I was studying arts in a small college in Montclair, New Jersey. There I fell in love with and married a young man, Marc Silverman, who wanted to become a physicist, but who suffered from cancer of the lymphatic system. He had been diagnosed with it when he was eighteen.

When I'd met him for the first time, he was twenty-one and I was eighteen. We both were in evening school together. Initially, he did not want to get involved with me as the doctors had told him that he had only two more years to live. But then we decided to defy logic and try to spend the little time we had joyfully, without worrying about the future. We wanted to feel love and not give up on life, even if it was limited. Our logic won. We went on to spend thirteen wonderful years together.

On finishing our studies, we planned to first pay a visit to my parents in India and from there start our journey to see the world. Before settling down, we both wished to explore the world. We were still very young and needed life experiences to know how to live our lives. On returning from this journey I expected to study with a well-known artist named Ed Harding, who lived in Northern Indiana. He had accepted me as an apprentice for a period of two years. It was a great opportunity for me. He was a strict teacher. He had seen a lot of potential in my works and saw great hope in me. I knew that it would be hard work, but I was still excited. I was eagerly looking forward to this part of my near future. My husband, Marc, who was later renamed Chinmaya by Bhagwan, was also happy about this opportunity. Though, by then, he himself had no idea of what he wanted to do in life.

As we waited for Chinmaya to take his final exams, I received a letter from my parents. My mother was in the hospital. She needed an eye surgery. I wanted to be close to her and take care of her. I had never seen my mother sick. She had always taken care of us so well that my desire to be with her when she was ill was very strong. Since I was finished with school, I decided to fly to India by myself the very next day. Chinmaya was to then follow immediately after his final exams and meet me at my parents' home.

It was a wonderful reunion with my parents. I surprised them on a cool December morning. We had not seen each other for five years. There was much love and joy in the air.

After visiting my mother in the hospital, I, according to her wish, accompanied my father on a trip to Bombay. There he had an important business appointment. He had almost never travelled anywhere without my mother ever since their wedding. On that trip, she could not accompany him because of her operation.

Coincidentally, Bhagwan lived just opposite the villa of my cousin where we were staying while in Bombay. So my wish to meet Bhagwan again was fulfilled. This meeting was an end and, at the same time, a beginning for me. I count it as one of the most important moments of my life. I was very excited.

We went to see Bhagwan without an appointment. His home was a three-room apartment in a high-rise building. His secretary Ma Yoga Laxmi (everybody called her Laxmi or Ma Laxmi) welcomed us from behind her desk, which stood at the entrance of the apartment.

"Ma," which means mother in Hindi, was the title given by Bhagwan to all female Sannyasins, because every woman has the potential of motherhood. Each male Sannyasin got the title of "Swami," as a reminder that everyone needs to master themselves.

Laxmi—that's how I addressed her when I got to know her better— was a small, petite woman who probably weighed no more than forty kilos. She looked very fragile. Her clothing consisted of a bright orange lungi, a kind of sarong worn by people in southern India, and a red kurta. She wore a red scarf over her head, like the hood of a nurse or a nun. Around her neck was a *mala* with a photo of Bhagwan. Her body appeared weak, but she walked, spoke, and moved with great energy. Her voice had strength. Her behaviour radiated confidence. She appeared astute and authoritarian. All this was not unpleasant for me. I did not feel threatened by her. She welcomed us with a broad smile and much warmth. She treated my father very respectfully, as if she had known him for a long time.

Normally Bhagwan did not receive anybody without an appointment. But, unusually and also fortunately, Ma Laxmi did not send us away that day. She led us into the living room that served as the office as well as the library and asked us to wait.

It was an impressive library, the only room in the apartment to which visitors had access. Three of its walls were covered up to the top with thousands of colourful books. The fourth wall consisted of windows. A fresh breeze was blowing in from the sea. The books and the fresh air made me forget that I was in the middle of a dirty and polluted city like Bombay. The noise of the outdoors was absent here. We were absorbed in the silence of the premises.

Ma Laxmi went and asked Bhagwan whether He wanted to see us. A few minutes later, my father and I were guided to His room. Bhagwan sat with crossed legs in a comfortable armchair in one corner of the room. He was wearing a white wrap. Beside Him stood a small table on which several books were lying. Opposite His chair were two beds. Apart from this the room was empty.

When I entered the room, Bhagwan looked at me, smiled brightly, and opened His arms. He invited me to come up to Him. I let myself fall into His arms, full of joy. He held me to His chest for some time. It seemed like an eternity. Then He let go of me gently and held my hands. I put my head on His lap. Then I looked at Him with a completely dissolved heart and a melting look. Bhagwan began to talk with my father. And I just sat there, drowned in Him, lost in Him. I heard everything that was spoken, and yet I heard nothing. I was there and yet I was not there.

That was it. It was the end. He and His feet were the last stop in my life. There was no other place I could go to after Him. Suddenly, I did not want to be without Him. It was no longer possible to remove Him from me. I could only talk about Him. He, and feelings and thoughts about Him, occupied me completely. I could not sleep. I could not eat. I could wait no longer. And I wished that Marc-Chinmaya, my first love, also get to know Him.

The same evening, I was invited to a lecture by Bhagwan. I could not wait until it was finally evening. It was the longest day of my life. The discourse was held in His living room which was filled with hordes of books. In this room there was space for about sixty to eighty people. That evening there were more people than that.

I would not have missed the discourse for anything in the world. We sat with our backs to the rear wall. I waited impatiently to see His beautiful eyes again. Bhagwan came from His bedroom and went very quietly through the room, His hands folded in *namaste*.

He wore a white robe, which reached down to His feet. A cloth napkin was lying on His shoulder. When He appeared, the audience became silent immediately. One could have heard even a pin drop in the quietness that thereafter descended on the room.

He stopped beside me. He asked me to come with Him and sit down in the front close to Him. I was overwhelmed. I followed Him. He pointed at His feet, and I sat down there, only a few inches away from Him.

There was nothing between us. There were no obstacles. I did not dare to blink my eyes; I was afraid that He might disappear. I just wanted to drink Him through my eyes. It felt as if He spoke only to me. All others did not exist anymore. There was nobody else, just Him and me. I could understand everything He said. I needed nothing else. He concluded His lecture, ". . . enough for today." It was enough for me. It was just right for me.

I sat glued to the spot until other people came up to Him, wanting to touch Him. In order to not disturb Him, I just wanted to quietly sneak out. I slowly walked to the door, music sounding in my ears. Then He called me back.

"Seela, you come and see me again tomorrow at 2:30 p.m." Then He turned to His secretary and said, "Laxmi, make sure that Seela comes to see me." Then He put His hand on my head and left.

Everyone looked at me in amazement. I felt their gaze upon me. I was vigorously excited. I could see Him again. I nearly became crazy. What should I wear? I wanted to look beautiful.

That night was the longest night of my life. I could not wait until it was 2.20 pm. I did not want to look at any clock. They were just not running fast enough. It seemed to me as if all the clocks in the world had stopped.

Finally the long-awaited moment arrived. It had been worth the wait. He looked even more beautiful than the previous day. I told Him that I could not sleep anymore, could not eat anymore, that I felt as if I were mentally ill. He just laughed and said, "Seela, it is quite simple. You are very much in love with me, and I am in love with you."

He was right. I *was* in love with Him.

During this meeting, I spoke with Bhagwan about death.

Chinmaya had cancer and it was incurable. The doctors had predicted that he had only a short time to live. Death was hovering over our heads like a naked sword, ready to fall down on us anytime. Chinmaya had not *really* lived and it was already time for him to die. It appeared simply unfair. He, a sensitive young man, had been unable to accept it. He wanted to understand death, but nobody would tell him anything about it. Nobody wanted to talk to him about death. Everyone was afraid.

Something Chinmaya and I had decided was that death would not be the end of our love. Death would not prevent us from being together. We had intensified our togetherness with these emotions.

This situation provided a well-prepared soil for the message of Bhagwan. He talked to me openly about death. He explained that we were lucky to see death hover over our heads. Death is a part of life, but most people forget it, He said. They don't want to know anything about it. But we were in a situation where it was impossible to ignore death. We were lucky. Bhagwan advised that we learn to see death as the culmination of life and not as the undesirable end. We should wait for death as we'd do for a welcome guest. We should expect it joyfully, like a lover, rather than encountering it with despair.

I understood what Bhagwan was saying. It made sense to me. I immediately wanted to bring Chinmaya to Him. I knew Bhagwan would be able to explain to him what death meant and that Chinmaya was intelligent enough to understand Bhagwan. He was going to arrive in Bombay in fifteen days. Those fifteen days seemed to me like one fifty.

Chinmaya was a young man with a scientific mind. He was sensitive, but also very logical. He was funny and sweet, but lazy. We fit together well. We liked to be together. It had been love at first sight for us. Chinmaya and I had been inseparable from each other for four years.

When he landed in Bombay, Chinmaya was overjoyed at seeing me again because he had missed me. I had not told him about Bhagwan and my new-found spiritual life. When he came to know about it, he was excited that something new was coming into his life. He was very understanding and immediately accepted my craziness.

On the day of his arrival, I took him to Bhagwan. Chinmaya was impressed by Bhagwan's intellect but did not react to any other aspect of His teachings. Bhagwan invited us to participate in a ten-day meditation camp. It was to take place near Bombay and was called Anand Sheela Meditation Camp.

Neither of us knew anything about meditation at the time. I did not even understand what the word meant. I was after something else. I was sure that my world would end with Bhagwan. He had become everything to me. He was the only interest I had. Chinmaya agreed to go the camp as he was always ready for new experiences. And because I was happy and wanted to be with Bhagwan, he was even excited about the camp.

The site of the camp was pretty run-down. The nearest human settlement was more than thirty kilometers away. There was no public transportation to reach the site. The organizers and some of the wealthy participants from Bombay had private cars. Everyone else had to arrange their transport separately.

The site had been donated to Bhagwan by one of His rich disciples to create a university for meditation. It was a useless piece of land. Maybe the owner just wanted to get rid of it.

Fortunately, we were modern American travellers who travelled well prepared. We took along our own tent and everything we needed. We erected our tent under one of the three trees that stood on the site. One was located next to Bhagwan's house; the second was next to the catering tent. Our tree was furthest from the activities of the camp. Perhaps that is why nobody had occupied it before us. Other than the three tree-shaded spots, there was only dust, and rocks. It was scorching hot.

But the environment was not of much interest for me. For me only Bhagwan existed. Chinmaya was happy to be with me, though we felt like strangers among the other participants. We had no idea about Bhagwan's work and had not bothered to research about either Him or His work. We were only there because He had invited us.

I felt as though I were on another planet. Language, dress, behaviour, everything was different and unusual there. That culture was unknown to us. We were there, but we did not really belong there. We were not Sannyasins. Nevertheless, we received special attention from Bhagwan. We were a hot topic of gossip among the Sannyasins.

Traditionally, Sannyasin means somebody who has renounced the world and who has embarked on an inner journey, the journey into the unknown. Society and its values mean nothing to this person. A Sannyasin is committed to the search for the real truth.

Bhagwan called the people He initiated "neo-Sannyasins."

He said: "My people will not have to renounce worldly things, but accept them and move beyond them. They live in this world and so they will affirm life and not deny it. They will enjoy life."

Through His new concept of Sannyas, He wanted to abolish the corruption then existing in spiritual pursuits and the deep-rooted Indian tradition of negating life. He wanted to encourage His Sannyasins to accept life while still pursuing their spiritual quests.

Sannyas is no gradual development; it is a quantum leap into trust. Sannyas is lottery, not trade. Sannyas is a willingness to blow out the candle of the ego. It is a feeling: "Now I am a disciple and I know nothing. I have left everything to my master. When he says, 'Wear orange,' then I will wear orange. When he says, 'Walk naked in the street,' then I will walk naked in the street. I know no other reasons for what I do. To find out why I do what I do, you must ask my master, because he has become my absolute guide. I have abandoned my self-determined lifestyle." This is the meaning of Sannyas, a complete and total surrender of ego to the master.

Bhagwan gave each of His Sannyasins a Mala—a necklace made of wooden beads and a locket. The locket contained on both sides a photo of Bhagwan. Every Sannyasin was required to wear this necklace. He also gave each Sannyasin a new name—the Sannyas name—so they could break with the identity of their pasts. This name symbolized their rebirth. He wanted His people to dress in orange, red, and all the colours of the sunrise. This clothing had to be loose and flowing to support the movement of energy in the body. It represented the rising sun. To be with Bhagwan meant to start the journey of meditation to higher levels of consciousness.

Bhagwan gave His lectures in both Hindi and English. Four times a day, He led the meditations. It was a feast of joy for my eyes to see Him this often. During the meditations I was a pain for the helpers. They had instructions to ensure that all meditators kept their eyes closed. But I did not want to close my eyes. When they'd come to me to order me to close my eyes, Bhagwan would signal them to leave me in peace. He knew why I did not want to close my eyes. It would have been too painful for me to be not allowed to see Him. To see Him and take Him in was more important for me than to meditate. To love made more sense to me than to jump up and down and call it meditation. Some people might not understand this. But this had more to do with feeling than with understanding. Only one who has loved will be able to understand me and my longing to drink Him with my eyes. I had no other choice. The only way open for me was to melt into Him.

On the second day of the meditation camp, I went to visit Bhagwan. Red is my favourite colour. I look very beautiful in it. It suits my skin colour. I wanted to look beautiful for Him. So I dressed in red. When Bhagwan saw this, He said with a broad smile, "My Seela looks beautiful in red. Which name do you want to have?" He put the Mala around my neck.

Totally confused out of love I replied, "Whatever you want."

He repeated laughingly, "Hmm . . . Whatever I want?"

I nodded with a glance. He took a writing case with His stationery and pen. He wrote His name on it and then scribbled the date and His signature underneath it. Handing me the sheet, He asked me with a mysterious smile, "Do you like the name Anand Sheela? Your new name is Ma Anand

Sheela." Anand means Joy, and Sheela was already my name; it means "one with a strong character." So I gladly accepted my new name.

Many years later, after I left Bhagwan, many thought that I would take back my old name. Many other Sannyasins had done that. I could never understand that. I had received this name in love. It was a gift from Bhagwan. This gift, which was given to me in love, I will not return. It makes no sense to take back my old name. That will not bring me back to who I was before I met Bhagwan. I also do not want to go back. The journey of my life leads forward, not backward. I know many who think that they can solve problems by taking back their old name again and behaving like before. I think that if they can do that, then they were never really with Bhagwan. Above all, I believe they never understood what He was all about. They never learned anything.

After giving me my new name, Bhagwan turned to Marc, who was accompanying me and had been watching everything closely in order to understand what was happening. He used to watch everything and figure things out using a logical approach. Bhagwan tried to put a Mala around Marc's neck too, but Marc withdrew laughingly and said, "No . . . no."

Bhagwan was not perturbed by this. He simply turned to me and said, "Seela, you seduce Marc to take Sannyas." Then He told Marc earnestly, "In two days you will be back to take Sannyas."

And so it was. I am not sure if I made him do it or whether it was because of the impact of Bhagwan's lecture—given in English—the next day. Everything He said touched Marc. It agreed with his logic and his mind. He became ready. He had to try this medicine or meditation, whatever it was that Bhagwan was offering. His new name was Swami Prem Chinmaya—loving consciousness—or just Chinmaya as he was referred to from then on.

10
Bhagwan and me: A journey begins

Our journey with Bhagwan began without any plan. We did not think much about it. He told us to let go, so we let go. That made things a lot easier for us.

Bhagwan began to play with us to find out how far we were ready to go with Him. He did that with everybody by making exceptional demands. He told us to travel in the middle of winter to Pahelgam, Kashmir, in order to meditate there for three weeks. Pahelgam is a well-known place at around three thousand meters in the mountains north of Srinagar in Kashmir. It is bitterly cold and often impossible to get to due to heavy snowfall. He knew well how difficult it would be to meditate in this cold. Most hotels there were closed that winter. Food was scarce. No heating, no comfort. The streets were blocked by a thick blanket of snow. Bhagwan saw this assignment as a test. But this was not a problem for us. We followed His instructions without any question. We stayed three weeks in Pahelgam and felt Bhagwan's presence in every movement, every action. We trusted Him without the slightest doubt and could therefore survive those exhausting days without complaining. We came back feeling superb—we had passed His litmus test with flying colours.

Next, He asked us to fly back to America and wind up the lives we were living there. This action whirled up many intense feelings among the members of our families. They thought that we were crazy and were destroying our future. Chinmaya's father threw him out of the house. He would have preferred a criminal son than a son walking around in an orange sarong. He also forbade his wife from talking about their son in the house. She was also not allowed to visit us, and, as time went by, we were also not allowed to visit her. She suffered from not being able to see her son. Later she managed to talk her husband into at least allowing us to visit her in the kitchen, which we could do using the backdoor. He accepted this because he never went into the kitchen.

My relatives were a little more civilized in their reaction. They explained to me how stupid it would be to forego my career as an artist and the training offered by Ed Harding, the artist in Indiana. All of them asked me to reconsider the decision Marc and I had made. My brother-in-law, my eldest sister's husband, behaved the worst on hearing about our decision. He thought he was an authority on truth and religion. He looked down on both of us and felt we were being stupid joining a commune like this. The irony is that today he belongs to the so-called inner circle of the very same commune! This smacks so much of hypocrisy. He eventually abandoned his family and his responsibility towards his two children to pursue the mirage of enlightenment and power and influence in the commune.

Only my father supported me against all opposition. He

understood my desire to remain near Bhagwan. He genuinely felt I could learn a lot from Him. My mother was at times worried as she was concerned about my future. Once she saw my father's approach, she too did not say much. Bhagwan started to show even more interest in us when we returned to India after effacing our lives in America. It was a significant proof of our commitment to Him. Until then He had only toyed with us. Now that He was sure that we wanted to walk the path of His vision, He started impelling us to move forward with Him. The time to prepare us properly had come.

In Bombay, Bhagwan was not very discriminating. He was then like a small river, only a short distance away from its source, touching every rock, every piece of debris that was on its way. At that time He was not very selective. He allowed everybody to see Him, and received almost everybody. He was looking for a few selected people with whom He could start His work. He chose them Himself. He did not care who those people had been, where they came from, and in what condition they had spent their lives. He was absolutely open and available. He gave almost everybody the chance to learn and grow near Him. The criteria for His choice were simple: love, trust, talents, and speed of learning.

The structure of His organization was loose. He wanted to work with everyone who was ready to work with Him. He segregated them by their performance and abilities and undertook this process in a very businesslike manner. So, there were talented people who could edit His books or translate His discourses. Then there were wealthy ones who could donate money or other expensive equipment that He required. Still others did petty physical work like cleaning His room or washing His clothes. Whenever He saw any potential in somebody, He gave them a chance. Those who took this opportunity came closer to Him. He was not interested in the others who were hesitant or not willing to commit totally.

During the first two years of His stay in Bombay, He began to give shape to His teachings. He started as a travelling philosopher after being thrown out of the University where He was teaching philosophy. He did not want to conform to the traditional rules and constrained thinking forced on Him there. He was known and respected among His students for His rebellious attitude. He was also a danger to female students. Women who attended His lectures would get infatuated with Him. Their attraction was a constant problem for the rest of the professors, who would be jealous. Moreover, they did not like that His lectures were always popular and overcrowded even though He taught a very dry subject—philosophy—and that even the students not enrolled in His class would bunk their other classes to listen to Him.

From 1966 to 1970 Bhagwan travelled throughout India. In 1970 He settled in Bombay, where many intellectuals, businessmen, and influential personalities open to new ideas and new ways of thinking lived. There He could start His career as an enlightened master.

Initially, He called Himself Acharya Rajneesh (teacher or professor), but later He took a giant step by taking on the audacious title of Bhagwan Shree Rajneesh, which literally means an incarnation of God.

In one breath He would talk about both sex and awareness. Consequently, He soon had the reputation of a controversial holy man. His book *From Sex to Superconsciousness* caused an outcry of indignation in the public. It provoked a lot of orthodox Hindus. There was so much controversy that India's Parliament actually discussed banning it.

To attract different people Bhagwan talked about many different subjects. So His audience would always be very mixed. People of every age, every race, and every religion attended His discourses. This diverse group inevitably aroused curiosity and interest in the press and the public. Because of this and other controversies surrounding Him, Bhagwan soon became well known. One could not ignore Him. Whoever came in contact with Him either loved Him or hated Him. He always provoked a reaction. Nobody could be indifferent towards Him.

Around 1972 an increasing number of western tourists became attracted by this phenomenon called Bhagwan and He was always keen to have a large international audience. Typically after His public discourses there would be music and celebration for the audience. His western followers were always seated on the podium. During the celebration they would dance around Him on it, along with some selected Indian supporters. It was always an interesting and colourful event. I attended many of these discourses and really enjoyed them all.

A few months after I came to know Bhagwan, towards the end of 1972, a clearer structure started emerging around Him. He became more and more exclusive. His secretary Laxmi started to more carefully select His visitors. All new visitors were asked to participate in Dynamic Meditation before they were allowed to have an audience with Him. Bhagwan had developed this meditation Himself. It took place every morning at six o'clock on a very crowded Chowpatty Beach in central Bombay. This meditation was extraordinary. It gave the participants an opportunity to be crazy with awareness for a short period. People who felt close to Bhagwan or His teachings, or those who wanted to learn something about meditation attended this public event. Dynamic Meditation was developed so that the Sannyasins could learn to open up and relax. Most of His followers began their day with this meditation.

To be able to perform this meditation properly, it is important to understand its meaning. It consists of five stages of ten minutes each. Each stage is essential, as it prepares for the next. Total concentration is required for the entire act to be successful.

The first phase consists of chaotic, fast, and intense breathing through the nose (to prevent hyperventilation). People today are not free. They have a habit of clinging to everything. They hold air in their lungs and don't exhale completely. An infant inhales deeply into the lungs and then exhales. But as a child grows up, his breathing becomes more and more shallow. An infant is open to life, to all social, economic, political, and religious experiences. He takes them in with full consciousness. However, as he becomes more protective, possessive, and greedy through his interactions with his surroundings, his breathing changes. So this first stage of meditation is meant to restore the original breathing, deep into the lungs. The deep breathing cleans the energy channels blocked by suppressed energies such as greed, anger, violence, jealousy, sex, and negativity. Many serious stomach and heart diseases are caused by such suppression. This deep breathing not only purifies the energy channels but also goes directly to the navel, where one's sexual energy is stored. Inhalation represents life, exhalation death. Normally we disown death. This chaotic breathing prepares one to accept death. The fear of death lessens and relaxation begins to set in. The total accomplishment of this stage prepares one for the second stage.

The second ten minutes provide the opportunity to ventilate everything suppressed and hidden, when the breathing of the previous stage has loosened all barriers previously erected inside by repressed feelings and emotions. In the second stage, participants cry, dance, jump, laugh, and scream as much as they want. Then they feel lighter. These first two stages clean the blocked channels of suppressed emotions down to the navel.

During the third phase, one jumps up and down with raised hands. This intense activity is the drive that brings one closer to one's Buddha nature. While jumping, one shouts the Sufi mantra, "Hu! Hu! Hu!" This is an abbreviation of the question, "Who am I?" It is the most fundamental and final question that every seeker of truth asks. Since repeating the entire question can lead to futile efforts of the mind and can make the mind race even faster, only the abbreviation "Hu!" is used. This mantra has a direct impact on the navel area. It awakens the sexual energy and sets it in motion. It rises up.

In the fourth phase one is required to stand completely still as if frozen. No movement, however small, is allowed. Now the energy arising from the navel can flood the entire body. It moves through the heart to the head. A total state of relaxation stops the mind and allows the energy to overcome oneself.

During the fifth stage, you share this energy with the whole Existence. You dance, celebrate life, and feel grateful.

Dynamic Meditation can be a miracle treatment for the contemporary man. It allows one a few moments to live all madness and emotions. It is a good exercise for the body and offers peace and relaxation to the mind. It opens the heart, so that love can flow.

At night Bhagwan held public discourses. While some of these discourses took place outdoors or in a public lecture hall accessible to everyone, others were conducted in His apartment. At these events, one could see Bhagwan and sit close to Him. The number of listeners depended on the location. Sometimes there were just 100 to 120 visitors, and sometimes as many as 5000 to 8000 participated.

One day He asked Chinmaya and me to share an apartment in Bombay with three other Sannyasins—Teertha, Sagar, and Mamta. I was aghast: I would rather be homeless than live together with three complete strangers! Right then, I expressed my dislike openly. I immediately asked Bhagwan, "Who is this Teertha? I don't know him!"

I did not even have the desire to know him. Since my return from America, I had heard some awful rumours about him, and, on meeting him later, I had found him terribly unappealing. He really was not my type. I was not happy.

Teertha was the first well-known therapist from the West to come to Bhagwan. To examine his knowledge, Bhagwan allowed him to lead an aggression group—which later became popular as encounter groups—with us.

These group therapies were meant to bring out one's latent

aggression, but they eventually became a stage for Teertha to act out his pomposity. I attended one of these groups once. In our first session, we sat in a circle. In the centre was kept a big pillow. For one hour, we verbally and vigourously expressed all our unhappiness, discomfort, and hate to each other and, in general, on the pillow. Then we took a shower. For Chinmaya and me it was ugly. We had never been exposed to such verbal aggression in our lives. The two of us never attended any other group therapy after this one. When I narrated my experience to Bhagwan later, He laughed. He found it amusing.

I continued my tirade, "Bhagwan, why do you want me to live with them? I do not want to."

He replied, "Seela, simply do what I tell you. Do not worry. I will take care of you." I had no option but to accept His orders.

We were a strange group. It would have been uncomfortable and awkward just to sit in one room with this group, let alone share a cramped two-room apartment in a damp and unpleasant part of Bombay. The only good thing about this apartment was that it had a lot of windows, so we could constantly let in the fresh sea breeze. The stench of the sea did not bother me, because for me the imagined stench of our living together was much worse.

None of us knew Bhagwan's purpose for making us live so closely together in two rooms. But we accepted it all, because Bhagwan had instructed us. Following Him and His instructions—that was the only point on which we five agreed.

Each of us was on a different trip, but each of us had, in their own way, a connection with Bhagwan. We had all felt the commitment of such a connection and had the desire to strengthen it by following Him and learning through Him.

Let me briefly describe here each of us, and also the dynamics between us:

Teertha: Founder of the encounter groups. Known for his work in the field of modern psychology. Had a very high opinion of himself. He himself was half a guru and tried to satisfy all his desires very selfishly. He was ready to go to bed with every woman who showed interest in him—and surprisingly there were many of them.

Sagar: He was later rightly nicknamed British Sagar. He boasted about being a good Brit. He constantly competed with Teertha. He tried to ape Teertha but would constantly stumble and stub his toe against something. He desperately wanted to become someone special; it was annoying.

Mamta: Talked with an irritating French accent. A pretty blonde with large breasts. Her body often shook like leaves in the wind—an activity she thought would demonstrate her progress in the field of meditation. She used to annoy everybody with her wailing voice and her constant crying and freaking out.

Chinmaya: A sweet guy with a great sense of humour. Funny and loving. Everybody liked him. He talked with a gentle voice and was simple to deal with. Nobody had any reason to complain about him.

Sheela: Apart from Chinmaya nobody could stand her. For every small thing that did not suit her, she would run to Bhagwan and cry into His ears. But she came through with everything. Bhagwan let her do whatever she wanted. She hated meditation. She hated the apartment and especially the bedroom and the toilet. She did not like to listen to the moaning from Teertha's bed every night. The whole experiment was a torture for her.

Teertha, Sagar, and Chinmaya were editing Bhagwan's books. Mamta was transcribing them. I had no particular task, so I took on myself to take care of the household and the purchase of food. That kept me at some distance from these people.

Except Chinmaya and me everyone went to Dynamic Meditation every morning. For the two of us the most horrible things during this experiment were the meals. Though there was always enough food for five people available, Mamta, Chinmaya, and I would still be left hungry after each meal. Teertha was always the first to throw himself on the food, like a vulture. At the dinner table, he never thought of the others. He just piled half of the food on his plate. Sagar would be the next to go. And we three would be left staring at each other, left to share the sparse remnants. After each meal Mamta would go to her bed and weep. Sagar would go to sleep and Teertha outside to find a woman. Chinmaya and I usually would rest a bit and then go out to eat again.

It was very difficult. In that dormitory-like room, each of us took a corner for ourselves. Chinmaya and I shared a corner, because we were a couple. There was no privacy, no curtains or partitions. Everything was open.

Our living together in a community under His direction was Bhagwan's first experiment of this kind. It was a painful, unpleasant time for Chinmaya and me. I would not want to meditate. I also could not get used to the aggression group sessions. This kind of living together was not for me, I could not cope with it well. Fortunately, Bhagwan treated Chinmaya and me in a very gentle and protective way. He did not insist that we take part in all the activities. For this, I was grateful to Him.

Fortunately, this experimental commune was disbanded just as quickly as it had been started. Actually, a donor of the project stopped the whole experiment by discontinuing his donations. He had not liked something Bhagwan had said in one of His discourses. I was happy. Now I did not have to sleep in one room with Teertha and Sagar anymore and could peacefully eat alone with Chinmaya.

11
Birth of the Rajneesh Ashram in Poona

Soon, Bhagwan had had enough of Bombay. He had been living in a very small apartment. Now He was no more a private person, but a man of public interest. He was talked about as a saint, a holy man, a guru. Because of His controversial and provocative public discourses, it had become almost impossible for Him to leave His apartment without protection. His supporters as well as His enemies did not let Him enjoy His walks in peace. Besides, there was no fresh air in Bombay. His allergies and asthma worsened there. The extent of pollution in the city was not good for anybody. The monsoon rains were relentless and exhausting, and they would adversely affect the health of the visiting Sannyasins. As a result, most foreign Sannyasins suffered from various illnesses. In addition to all this, accommodations were also hard to find in the city and were generally very expensive.

Some very rich Sannyasins from Bombay did not want Bhagwan to leave Bombay, primarily for the selfish reason of their own convenience. But they also could not find a new home for Him where He could expand and live freely and comfortably to carry on His work.

The time had come for Him to move on. He could no longer wait. He was ready. His people were ready to go with Him to the farthest corner of the world. He told His secretary Laxmi to look for a large space in the vicinity of Bombay, the main business centre of India. For Him it was important that the facilities of a big city be nearby. He wanted good relations with the press and all other major media networks, as well as with large companies. Access to an international airport within close distance was important too. Availability of readymade infrastructure at the space where He could immediately continue His work was also critical. He apparently had a clear vision for the future. After an exhaustive search Laxmi found a suitable property in Poona, one that met most of these requirements.

The city of Poona (now Pune) is located approximately 160 km southeast of Bombay (now Mumbai). It is a smaller city than Bombay but has excellent universities, a well-managed municipality, and a much better climate. Weather, vegetation, and air are better in Pune than in Bombay. This city was ideal for Bhagwan and His vision. It was also close enough to the Bombay international airport. That was important because He wanted to focus more and more on the visitors from the West. For His purpose, Pune was exactly the right location, at exactly the right distance.

The unhappy and disappointed followers from Bombay blamed Laxmi for His departure from the city. They were convinced that Bhagwan had left Bombay against His will. They accused Laxmi of being power-hungry. Every secretary of Bhagwan seemed to have suffered this fate sooner or later.

A few years later I was also accused of exactly the same thing. To stand between Bhagwan and His people was not easy for Laxmi. It was like being at the ends of two opposing swords.

After moving to Poona, Bhagwan changed certain things within His organization. He took a clearer direction. He redefined His work anew and changed some fundamental things in His private and public life. With the help of His secretary Laxmi, He isolated Himself more. During this process He discarded all the people who were just hanging around uselessly. He made Himself more exclusive and ensured that He appeared more mysterious. Now, He did not meet as willingly as before with all those who wanted to see Him. Private meetings were stopped completely.

In the beginning, He would meet with several visitors in His garden. There He would sit in a lounge chair, which looked like a sofa. If He wanted to say something personal to somebody, that person was brought to Him before the whole group entered the garden. This happened only during the first weeks and months. Then an auditorium on one side of His house was built. There He gave His discourses in the morning and *darshan* (silent public appearance) in the evening. His private meetings now became public *darshans*.

It became increasingly difficult to get appointments with Him. He began to choose His visitors carefully. The meetings with Him took on a more formal character. He sought people He could rely on for following His instructions faithfully. He only wanted brave, dependable people around Him. He was looking for workers, not followers. He demanded complete surrender. Trust was the only basis for an association with Him. There was no room for doubt. There were enough of those who wanted to just remain and work on the surface. He weeded these people out, so that the real seeds of His vision were given a better chance to grow and blossom. He only needed people who were willing to risk everything. According to Him, the truth could not be learned without taking a risk. He chased away people mercilessly when He saw no potential in them. He needed hundred percent from everybody, and wanted to hear no complaints.

Foreigners got more and more attention from Him. He turned a cold shoulder towards most Indians. Not everyone was allowed to ask questions. He also pulled the rug from under the feet of the rich and demanding Indian supporters of the earlier days. They had expected that He would always be available to them because of their past financial support. But they were not prepared to grow. His words were their drug. He did not need such people. He did not want them any longer. He occasionally said about them, "These people are of no use. They are lazy and greedy. They have big egos . . . I cannot do anything with them. They only create problems . . ."

Sometimes He played subtle games to get rid of them. They, in turn, blamed His secretary Laxmi and were enraged with her. In Poona, from the very beginning, He gave her visibly more support and power. She became a wall between Him and the public. It was an important but thankless role. Slowly but surely, she became the target of accusations. Bhagwan used her as a buffer. She was clearly a puppet—His puppet. He pulled the strings in the background. He worked through Laxmi. He gave her precise instructions for every situation. She had to take care of all His worldly affairs. To be trained by Him was a very rare opportunity. No university could provide such a good education. Whoever wanted to learn from Him had to learn in every moment. Each second was like an entire semester. I also got this gift later. The wisdom of my father proved correct. He had told me once, when I was a young girl, "What you can learn from this man in a few discourses would otherwise take many lives." So it was.

I sometimes have the impression that I am several hundred years old. I often joke when people ask me how old I am. I say, "At least 380 years old." It feels like that. The learning and the rich life experience with Bhagwan make me feel this old.

This wealth can never be lost. This treasure no one can steal. The price for this was: unconditional surrender, and love without demands, without expectations.

He told His secretaries to be tough and strict. He allowed no negativity, no complaints. The times of courting people to come to Him, as in Bombay, were gone. Now He would tell us to get ourselves moving. He made it clear to us that we had to either become better or go. Uncertain behaviour was no longer accepted.

This new attitude caused dissatisfaction among many long-time supporters. It also became a problem for those who had come with their own ideas, opinions, and agendas. He wanted no advice. He was the one to give advice.

He let everybody know clearly who the master was.

12
Implementing Bhagwan's vision of a new man

Everything happening around Bhagwan seemed to fulfill a purpose, even if at first glance it would not make any sense.

He loved craziness and bragging. That made the government angry and also disturbed the Sannyasins. Bhagwan often staged things that caused trouble, planning everything in advance down to the smallest detail. His perception of people and their skills was immense. Everyone felt totally naked when they sat in front of Him. Nothing could be hidden from His piercing look. It was a good thing that I loved Him unconditionally. I had nothing to hide from Him.

He often took advantage of people's weaknesses for His own purposes. It did not bother Him to be seen as a brute, as long as His objectives were achieved. He was a man without limits.

For a long time Bhagwan had a plan for how to carry out His work on a grand scale. He did not want to let anything, especially practical considerations, come in the way of realizing His dream of creating a New Man. For the development of the New Man, He needed a big commune and the right environment. He needed a grand ashram.

An ashram is neither a school, nor an institution of formal learning. It is a refuge where disciples live with an enlightened master and learn life's lessons from him. It is a place where one can live and work under the direct guidance of the master and his energy field. An ashram exists around an enlightened master. Once the enlightened one is not there the ashram disappears. What is then left is only the organization, the skeleton. The master, the enlightened one, is the soul of the ashram.

Bhagwan knew exactly how to create situations for keeping away unwanted people. He would plan His actions carefully. For example, He could talk about Buddha, so that the unwanted followers of Mahavir would simply disappear. When He no longer wanted poor people and curiosity seekers to crowd the ashram in Poona, He decided to increase the entry fees for His discourses.

All of a sudden one day He began to give His discourses in English to drive away local Indian followers. For the locals this was a personal insult. When He left Bombay for Poona He, in order to snub the Bombay Sannyasins, intimated that they had not received Him well. He caught not just one or two, but many birds with one stone. He was a master in recognizing the peculiarities of the human mind.

He had developed a special vocabulary for His people. It was something very special and had its own meaning and values. These values distinguished His way of life, His philosophy, and His work from all others. The vocabulary also helped Him create a special atmosphere for His people. They were carried from the old to the new, away from their ordinary past to a new future. They were immediately placed in a new environment, so they were completely separated from their roots. Everything around Bhagwan served to break with old identities.

Words such as "surrender" and "enlightenment" stood at the top of the hierarchy, followed by "meditation," "faith," "love," and "trust." To arrive at the desired spiritual place, one had to meditate, attend His discourses, and participate in therapy groups. Each activity was designed to ensure that these defining concepts were understood, felt, and freely expressed in everyday life. Everything served to bring the Sannyasins closer to themselves, to make them look into their own being. They were kept busy from morning till night. Most hours of the day were filled with intense activity. The daily timetable consisted of hard work for the workers, and therapy groups and meditation for the visitors.

The ashram took on the appearance of a beautiful campus, surrounded by green gardens and trees. People were happy to find such a quiet zone in the middle of India. It was a peaceful cynosure with no beggars, no street vendors, no hashish sellers. They found a nice environment with an exciting colourful atmosphere, interesting people, and an interesting life. It was a paradise that could be enjoyed by people from the West and India alike. It helped them relax and drop their anxieties. There was an opportunity to look inside oneself, to peer into one's own being. It was a good place to move from the outer, ordinary world to the inner one. Here one could forget everyday problems.

The organization served to create and foster Bhagwan's dream of the New Man. Bhagwan had set it up to let conflicts arise. Conflicts were considered a good tool to go deeper inside by Him. According to Him, conflicts should become visible and tangible, and not be suppressed or pushed under the surface. Only thus can they serve inner growth. Bhagwan would often praise a Sannyasin publically whom He thought of as financially resourceful, and sometimes He'd blame the organization for something—even if we were only following His orders—just to pacify a person with resources. He would often ask Laxmi or me in private to do just the opposite of what He had just said in public. He would explain to me that people need their egos patted, otherwise they would not work. Such situations were often related to money.

The organization gave Him financial benefits too. He was very clever when it came to donations. For instance when it was convenient, He separated Himself from the organization and claimed He had nothing to do with it. At other times, He claimed He was in public silence even though He worked with me for hours each day, telling me how and what to do. At the same time He would declare not knowing the working of the organization. As far as the public was concerned, Bhagwan could not be giving any orders as He was in silence. The organization was seen by many as Laxmi and Sheela's trip. For His followers, Bhagwan could never do any wrong. Some people were more willing to donate money for His personal needs than for the organization. Through donation they wished to come closer to Bhagwan.

The leaders of His organization had understood His approach and method from the beginning itself. So, they tolerated these conflicts and, in due course of time, got accustomed to His way of working.

Everything that happened around Him was interconnected.

If somebody wanted to learn, the opportunity to learn was present in every minute. If somebody liked to complain, he could spend his whole life complaining. If someone was negative, he could swim all day long in a cesspool of negativity. If one wanted to lose oneself in intellectualism, one could do this for as long as he wanted to. For everybody there was an opportunity to learn and grow in all dimensions. One could experience heaven or hell, be a saint or a charlatan. It depended on the individual's own make-up.

A warrior came to the Zen master Hakuin and asked "Is there such a thing as heaven and hell?"

Hakuin said "Who are you?"

The warrior replied "I am chief samurai to the emperor."

Hakuin said "You, a samurai? With a face like that, you look more like a beggar."

At this the warrior became so angry he drew his sword.

Standing calmly in front of him, Hakuin said "Here open the gates of hell."

Perceiving the master's composure, the soldier sheathed his sword and bowed.

Hakuin then said "And here open the gates of heaven."

(From "The Gates of Heaven and Hell," in *Osho: A Bird on the Wing*)

From the very first step they took in the ashram, the Sannyasins were shown their place. Bhagwan always sat in a chair and all others sat at His feet. They, full of trust and devotion, would surrender to Him. True learning could only happen when there was devotion. Doubts were not tolerated.

Doubts and negativity were taken very seriously and corrected immediately. Bhagwan once said, "If you go to a doctor and ask for help because you are sick, then you need to trust that he would give you the right medicine. Take his help. Do not say that you know yourself what is best for you. Take the medicine . . ."

He was right. He did not like it if somebody came with an attitude that he already knew everything. One should go empty to a master. Only thus can he fill one with his knowledge, with the truth of life. Bhagwan once told a wonderful story about a Zen master.

A professor of philosophy went to a Zen Master, Nan-in, and asked about God, about nirvana, about meditation, and so many things. The Master listened silently – questions upon questions from the professor. Then he said, "You look tired. You have climbed this high mountain; you have come from a faraway place. Let me first serve you tea." And the Zen Master made tea. The professor waited. He was boiling with questions. And when the Master was making tea and the samovar was singing and the aroma of the tea started spreading, the Master said to the professor, "Wait, don't be in such a hurry. Who knows? Even by drinking tea your questions may be answered... or even before that."

The professor was at a loss. He started thinking, "This whole journey has been a waste. This man seems to be mad. How can my question about God be answered by drinking tea? What relevance is there? This man is a madman. It would be better to escape from here as soon as possible because who knows how and what he is going to do next. And the crazy master says: 'Even before that, who knows, your questions may be answered?'"

But he did not leave immediately; since he was feeling tired and thought it would be good to have a cup of tea before he started descending back down the mountain.

The Master brought the kettle, poured tea in the cup – and went on pouring. The cup was full, and the tea started overflowing in the saucer, but he went on pouring. Then the saucer was also full. Just one more drop and the tea would start flowing on the floor. The professor impatiently yelled, "Stop! What are you doing? Are you mad or something? Can't you see the cup is full? Can't you see the saucer is full?"

And the Zen Master said, "That's the exact situation you are in: your mind is so full of questions and thoughts that there is no room for my answer to go in. But you look like an intelligent man. You could see the point, that now even a single drop more of tea and it will not be contained by the cup or the saucer; it will start overflowing onto the floor. And I tell you, since you entered this house your questions are overflowing all over the place. Your head is small, but so full of your questions; go back, empty your cup, and then come. First create a little space in you."

(From "La Illaha Ill Allah," in *Osho: The Secret*)

In the daily routine of the ashram, Dynamic Meditation was followed by Bhagwan's discourses which aimed to impart both discipline and humour. They gave us the opportunity to sit with Him for one or two hours. For thousands of people who followed Him, these discourses were the most important event of the day. Through His lectures He encouraged us to go deeper into our hearts. He would say, "Leave your mind and your shoes outside . . ."

His discourses were the medium used to give us symbolic hits of the Zen-stick. During His discourses in front of a large gathering, He could either exalt a person with compliments, giving their egos a giant boost and increasing their confidence, or He could point out their weaknesses, making them feel smaller than a speck of dust. Anyone listening to His discourse had the feeling that Bhagwan was speaking only and directly to him. This art of speaking also showed that He was a great sales genius. He gently seduced us into letting go of our old values and taking on new ones. He pushed us onto the path whose destination was unknown. He propelled us onwards on an inward journey. That was His intention and His main job. He created trust in us. Through this trust we were able to surrender and could transform ourselves into His vision of a New Man.

The remaining activities of the day helped reinforce the qualities that He wanted us to develop. Everyone used the same expressions of our own special vocabulary. We all felt like a big family. There was a certain uniformity in our collective existence. We were taught that we must not be fragmented individuals. The purpose of life in the ashram was to become whole, to be complete.

He tried to enforce this purpose even through our clothing. After our initiation into Sannyas we could wear only the colours of the sunrise. That served to remind us that we were a part of a growth process, on a journey into our inner world, that we were no longer ordinary.

Our clothing was loose. During the initial days it consisted of only one piece. This was to facilitate the movement of energy within the body and to prevent the unconscious from dividing the energy into upper and lower areas. Upper areas of the body were accepted by most established religions. However, the lower part of the body was seen as dirty by many as it is linked to sexuality. As a result it was suppressed and never talked about. But in Bhagwan's ashram it was important to be integrated and not be divided into upper and lower parts. Everything that happened around Bhagwan had a reason behind it. Everything was directly related to His work and His vision.

13
The exploitation of Sannyasins begins

Once Bhagwan established Himself in Poona, more than five thousand people began to come to listen to Bhagwan every day. Thousands came by plane from the West to India just to be with Him. Because of the Rajneesh ashram in Poona, Indian tourism achieved growth rates exceeding fifteen percent. The ashram was also responsible for bringing Poona onto the world map. Most tourist guides in the West even began to publish information on Poona and the Rajneesh ashram.

Our presence also gave greater stability to Poona's economy. In an economically fragile time, the businessmen in Poona got a very handsome source of income. Our foreign visitors spent money generously. We brought wealth and colour to the city.

For the expansion of the ashram much money was needed. Bhagwan did not want to be dependent on donations any longer. That was too risky and nettlesome. Those who offered money linked their gifts to conditions. As long as their egos were massaged, there was money. Bhagwan was not interested in doing this. He told us regularly that time was running short.

What can be done tomorrow should be finished today. There was no tomorrow for Him. It was now or never.

He wanted to quickly expand His work. His aim was to create a new human being, Homo Novus—a New Man who lives at his highest potential, the potential of Buddha. He is not split inside between the physical and the spiritual, but is whole and complete. Bhagwan taught that there is a synthesis between Zorba and Buddha. Zorba represents the earth and life, while Buddha stands for divine awareness. The meeting of the two is a meeting of heaven and earth. Bhagwan wanted to dissolve the polarities between man and woman, yin and yang, summer and winter. He wanted to bring together Sex and Samadhi.

The New Man is courageous, not hypocritical or dishonest. He is authentic. He does not create a jail around him and live like a prisoner; instead he enjoys total freedom. He is filled with life, love, and joy. This New Man knows no boundaries between people of different colours or ideologies. He is universal, not bound by creed, religion, or nationality. He is neither a capitalist nor a communist; rather he is just a man who cannot be put into a specific box. He is a complete man.

Bhagwan was also a good businessman. He knew His products, their value, and their market. He wanted the ashram to work such that all costs were covered. An entrance fee hence began to be asked for His discourses. His group therapists also went into action. In the ashram therapies began to be offered as food is on a buffet. Visitors could pick and choose and pay for their choice. The ashram also started other fee-based services for the visitors and group participants. Money began to flow like water.

During the early '70s, group therapies used to play a major role in the psychology of the Western people. To them, therapies seemed to be the answer to the dissatisfaction of modern man. Among educated people, it was the in thing to participate in group therapies. In some circles, it was even regarded as old-fashioned to have no experience with such therapies. People decorated themselves with them as though they were medals. Some even became really addicted to these therapies.

The therapy groups were to help release the anger, hate, jealousy, sexual suppressions, and other taboos that one learns and carries through life. Bhagwan thought that once a person is free of these unpleasant feelings, one can move towards inward journey easily. There were many different types of therapies offered at the ashram. Only encounter groups dealt with aggression and were perhaps the most popular therapy group.

Sexuality, which was seen as the cause of many sufferings, was one of the main topics in these therapies. The liberation of repression and sexual perversion was their focal point. Sexuality was accepted without judgment. There were no taboos, no moral issues attached with sexuality. Bhagwan wanted us to be free of jealousy and possessiveness. He wanted us to deal with our sexuality by acting it out with the consent of the partner. He wanted us to go beyond moral and guilt restraints. There was a lot going on in these groups. Some, in the excitement of the group and the enthusiasm to climb the ladder of enlightenment took part in violence and sexual encounters in groups. But always, the participation was absolutely voluntary.

In India, these therapies were a complete unknown. People had no idea how they worked. The locals who feared the unknown were frightened of them. To prevent this fear from spreading everywhere, Indians were not allowed to participate in therapy groups in the ashram. This seemed like discrimination to the Indians. But some of the therapies *were* truly frightful. Occasional bone fractures and black eyes were normal.

Not everyone understood why Bhagwan banned Indians from participation in these groups. Many questions were put to Him about this. Finally, He gave an official reason so that the negativity did not spread further. He said, "People from the West come from a very oppressive world. Their lifestyle is different from that of an Indian's. Their mindset is different. They need active therapies. Indians need more passive, quiet meditations . . ." With this explanation the Indians thought they were more spiritually developed.

With this feeling of spiritual superiority, some of the Indian Sannyasins began to walk around with their noses in the air. But the real reason for Bhagwan's statement was that He did not want the local Indian sentiment to turn against Him with accusations of discrimination. By excluding Indians from the whole exercise, He also made sure that no ugly gossip was spread. The ashram needed to prevent the Indian authorities from discontinuing the therapies. A ban on therapies would have been very bad for the business. The ashram depended on the continual cash flow generated by the therapies to support itself financially.

Bhagwan was very conscious of the economic value of the group therapies and therapists. He started to publicly show preference for the therapy leaders in order to flatter their egos. Like a clever businessman, He always showed strong personal interest in people who had a high economic potential. He knew that much money was needed for His work and to keep up His luxurious lifestyle. So, He would always massage the ego of these people by calling them highly developed, conscious beings. But, like always, when they became a plague, He would turn the tables on them. He was a master at taking advantage of people for their money or their skills. Afterwards, when they no more supported His intentions in a productive way, He would throw many of them out of the ashram. Bhagwan was very different from typical Indians who continue to consider a cow sacred long after it has stopped giving milk. Bhagwan had no scruples in sending a cow He could no longer milk to the slaughterhouse.

It was interesting to listen to how the Sannyasins talked about their therapies. It sounded as if without therapies there was no possibility of enlightenment for them—and to them *that* sounded like a major catastrophe. They compared records of who had done which therapy groups. They tried to find spiritual explanations for the sequence in which Bhagwan had recommended therapies to them. They could not see it as a simple, practical marketing and moneymaking process.

Bhagwan combined these therapies with meditation, so that they served His purpose. He had to sell them. He was the best salesman. After all, He had His customers secured. Nobody said no to Him. He could sell His people anything and everything. When He initiated a person as a Sannyasin, He at the same time recommended the participation in a sequence of group therapies. His proposals were accepted unquestioningly and in totality. Sannyasins took them as commandments, as a very important and necessary step towards their enlightenment.

Actually, to give His recommendations, Bhagwan always consulted a chart we would prepare for Him. On this chart, we highlighted the groups that were not sold out. He gave His recommendations according to the spaces available. Sannyasins would take this as a big spiritual theater and would measure the distance that still separated them from enlightenment by the number of completed groups. They calculated which level of spirituality they had already achieved.

These therapy groups were expensive. For many Sannyasins this was a problem. Many of us coming from the West had lived in India for years without any income. The savings had been used up long ago. So, many of us were very poor. To have money meant to be able to be in the ashram and with Bhagwan, and many of us were willing to become beggars rather than be separated from Him. Some even decided to work as prostitutes. To have money and be able to live with Bhagwan was more important than the method of accumulating money.

Bhagwan's teachings did not preach any morality. This made it easy to overcome guilt in these matters. The only valid guilt was related to Him. Bhagwan would often say that life as a prostitute can be important in the spiritual quest. Like many of the ancient Tantric teachers He would say, ". . . prostitution can serve as a kind of meditation. One can learn to observe how the body takes part in the sexual act when the consciousness of being exists separately. This is a good opportunity to be the watcher." He told many stories on this subject. He taught us not to judge, but to use every situation in life to develop awareness.

A great sage told one of his disciples to go to the court of the king and be there for a few days as his last lesson.

'If this is what the master wants...' The young man went. He thought, 'Perhaps the king is a great sage; he must be greater than my own master, if my master sends everybody to him for the last lesson and the last test.

'Strange that a sage who has renounced everything should send his disciples to a man who has not renounced anything, who is just an ordinary power-hungry man, continually trying to conquer other countries; an imperialist, so attached to things that he does not bother about killing thousands of people. And I am being sent to him? There must be some secret in it.'

He went there. It was evening time, and he was brought immediately before the king. It was time for the king to drink; beautiful women had come to dance. His court was now going to celebrate the evening.

Seeing all this, the young renunciate felt terrible, shocked, and he said to the king, 'I had come to stay for a few days but I cannot stay here for a few minutes even. I cannot think why my master has sent me to this hell!'

The king said, 'If your master has sent you, there must be some reason. And don't be so judgmental so quickly. What are you going to lose in two or three days' time? And remember, this is your last test. Without my approval you can remain there in your master's house your whole life, but you will never be declared graduate. So it is better that you come to your senses; remain here for three days. You have not been sent here to judge me; you have been sent here to be judged by me.'

Now, this was too much: this man was going to judge him, who had renounced everything! But what to do? He was in a fix. If he goes go back, the master will be unhappy. And if this was going to be the case, he will have to finally come back here. 'It is better to pass these three days somehow and get the clearance from this arrogant man,' he thought.

The king said, 'You are cooling down and coming to your senses. First take a good bath that I had prepared for you when the message of your arrival had come to me. But don't be worried: in youth everybody is too quick to judge. It takes a little experience not to judge, not to judge superficially at least. And you have not seen anything.

'Be here for three days, watch, see. Then you have your whole life there in which you can judge – no problem – but first get my clearance. So first think of how I'll judge you and move accordingly, so that you can get a favorable judgment from me; otherwise you will have to come here again and again and again, your whole life. So you go and take a bath – I have arranged everything.'

The young man had never been in the bath of a king before; he had never seen such a beautiful place. Naked women were there to massage him . . . He said, 'My God, this test is the end; in three days this man is going to kill me!' Three days was enough time for that. He could not speak any further. He was really on the verge of a nervous breakdown. All his life he had escaped from women and here he finds naked women right in front of him. Never before had he seen such beautiful women, and now they were going to give him a massage!

He could not say anything anymore, in fact he found he had lost his voice. He could only say 'Aaaahh!' – nothing more. Soon those women started undressing him. Before he could do anything, he was standing naked; those four women took possession of him completely and brought him to the bathtub which was filled with rose water.

In the East, kings and very rich customarily took baths in rose water. In the night, hundreds of roses were put in the bathtub so their fragrance is absorbed by the water. Then in the morning the flowers are removed, so you don't see many roses, but you are surrounded by a cloud of rose fragrance.

He had never in his whole life seen anything so luxurious. The bathtub was made of gold; precious oils were poured on his body and he was massaged. And he was dying to escape somehow from there, but he was feeling completely paralyzed.

And then the king invited him to a feast of things that he had never tasted before. He had always read: 'Discipline yourself to tastelessness' — and here was such tasteful, delicious food! Just the aroma, the flavor, was enough to make you go crazy.

The king said, 'Sit down and eat — and remember your discipline of tastelessness. What was the point in your master's house where the food was tasteless anyway? If you could remember tastelessness there, do you think that was because of some discipline? It was tasteless; any idiot would have felt tastelessness. Now try and feel tastelessness.'

The young man saw the difficulty but saw the point also. 'And by the way,' the king said, 'how was the bath? Were the women nice to you? They are the best out of all the masseuses. I think you must be feeling satisfied.'

He said, 'Satisfied? I am just somehow trying to get through the three days — if I can survive, but I don't have much hope. This is the first evening; three days seem like three lives to me. And now this food! I will not forget it my whole life — and I have to be a renunciate! And those beautiful women — I will not forget them. What kind of test is this? You are giving me all the experiences against which I have been prepared all these years.'

Then came the wine, and the king offered him some himself. The young man said: 'This is too much — wine is prohibited in my master's house.'

The king said: 'This is not your master's house, this is your examiner's palace. If you want clearance, be alert and do what I say. Your master has told you not to be unconscious. Don't be unconscious; drink and remain conscious. What is the point of remaining conscious without drinking? Anybody can do that; everybody is doing that.

'You better drink, and drink to your heart's content, because never again will you get this chance. And I tell you, consciousness has nothing to do with it: I will be drinking with you; in fact I have been drinking the whole evening – can you say I am unconscious? So drink!'

He had to drink. He was falling apart, not knowing what was happening – the intoxication, the women, the food, the beautiful clothes that were given to him after the bath . . . And then the king took him to the guesthouse where he was to stay. He could not believe it. He thought he must have come to heaven – alcohol gives many people the feeling of being in heaven.

Perhaps that's why all the religions are against alcohol, because if alcohol can satisfy your desire for heaven, who would bother to go to the churches and to the temples and do all kinds of strange things, when heaven is possible through the simple process of drinking alcohol?

The young man thought he must be in heaven; he forgot completely that he had come for his final test. The king showed him his bed, and the moment the young man lay down he saw a naked sword hanging by a thin thread just above him. All intoxication disappeared; suddenly he found that he was not in heaven. That sword . . . Death can bring anybody back to earth from anywhere!

He asked the king, 'Why is this sword hanging here?'

The king said, 'This is hanging here to keep you conscious. This is your room – now, go to sleep. And if, by God's grace, both of us survive till tomorrow morning, we will meet again.'

The young man said to the king, 'Nothing is going to happen to you, you will survive all right; the question is about me. Even with God's help I don't think this thin thread can hold this heavy, naked sword hanging over me; it is going to fall any moment. Just a little breeze is enough, and I am finished!'

The king said, 'Don't be worried. If you are finished off – your master must have been telling you about reincarnation – you will be reincarnated – a rebirth. And whatever you have learned will go with you. So don't miss these last moments. Perhaps it may fall – I cannot guarantee anything. It is up to you what you make of these moments. Remain conscious, and if you die in consciousness, nothing can be better than that.'

But the young man said: 'I don't want to die. I have come here just to get the clearance, and you are just clearing me away from life itself!'

The king said: 'This is the way one gets the clearance. You go to sleep: whatever is going to happen is going to happen – that's your master's teaching. That's what Hindus say: Even a leaf does not move without God's will, so how can a sword kill you without God's will? And WITH His will, sword or no sword, you will be killed.

'So just go to sleep, the way I go to sleep. Over you there is only one naked sword hanging; over me there are thousands of naked swords hanging. And yet, soon you will hear my snores from the other room.'

The young man could not sleep the whole night; the whole night he heard the king snoring. In the morning, the king came into his room. The young man was fully awake, lying, just looking at the sword; there was nothing else in the whole world except the sword.

The king said, 'I am going to take a bath' – just behind his palace was the sacred river Ganges. Come along with me for the morning walk, and a little swim in the river.' They went down to the river. The young man wore nothing except a small langoti, a traditional small loin cloth worn by Hindu monks draped around ones waist and between the thighs.

The young man came to the river wearing only the langoti, leaving behind the finer clothes the king had given.

He said: 'In the palace I can use them but not outside. If somebody sees me in these robes it will be very embarrassing for me and for you, so let me wear my everyday uniform of langoti.

The king said, 'That is up to you.' So the king went in his royal clothes and the monk in his uniform. They both put their clothes on the bank of the Ganges and entered the water. While they were taking their bath the monk shouted to the king, 'Your palace is on fire!'

The king said, 'I saw it before you did, but there is nothing to be worried about. Now what can be done? It is on fire, but nothing happens without God's will so don't be worried; you just take your bath.'

The young man said, 'What are you saying! At least I have to save my uniform that was lying by the side of the palace,' and he ran out of the water to save his uniform. The palace was burning, the king's clothes were lying there, but he was worried about his own loin-cloth!

The king took his bath. The palace was in ashes, completely destroyed – it had been set on fire on his orders. The monk was shaking and trembling, and he was saying, 'It is such a great loss. How many millions of rupees!'

But the king said, 'Don't worry; that has nothing to do with you. Your things are safe.'

The young man said, 'All my things are perfectly safe.'

The king said, 'That's enough for you – you should be worried about your things: these are your possessions, this is your kingdom. But I don't care if my whole kingdom burns down; it doesn't matter – because before when I was not here, the world was here and the kingdom was here. One day I will not be here again and the world will continue. I am here just as an observer. Why should I get too involved?

'But you have to remember that you have not been able to renounce anything; you have not yet become a detached observer. You could not even watch my house on fire. If your uniform – which is not much of a uniform – had been on fire I think you would have gone mad! You are *already in a state of madness because of so much loss . . . But what has it to do with you?*

'And you were shocked seeing me drinking, but you don't know that even while drinking I am a conscious observer. You were shocked seeing me surrounded by beautiful women; even looking at their dance I am only an observer. But you are not a detached observer at all. Now make up for it within two days. The time is short, very short. Be a detached observer, because before I give you the clearance so that you can graduate, you will have to prove that you have become a detached witness, an observer.'

He said, 'How have I to prove it?'

The king said, 'Today just go on trying it on everything. Everything is managed in such a way that it will help you watch. Just watch. Don't try to escape, don't try to repress, don't try to fight, don't try to avoid: just watch, let things happen.'

And on the last day, the last test was that there was going to be a beautiful dance. This young man was given a cup full of oil – so full that if he just moved a little, the oil would spill. The dancers were in a circle and the king was sitting in the middle. And the man, the poor young man holding that precious bowl full of oil, was told 'Even if a single drop of the oil falls, you have failed.'

Now there was so much temptation to look at on every side – so many beautiful women dancing! But from that bowl, just a single drop . . . just a single moment of unwatchfulness . . . He passed by the women, went around them – and as he was going around, slowly, slowly watchfulness settled in him. He forgot all about the dance; there was only the 'now,' the oil, and watchfulness . . .

(From "Exactly How Do You Do It?," in *Osho: From Misery to Enlightenment*)

Bhagwan had described to His management the value of the groups very clearly. "Remember, the groups are a good source of income. Once someone is allowed to participate for free, others will also want that. You must understand human nature. If people do not have to pay for something, they do not believe that they will receive any value from it. If they pay and do not get what they expected, they will say nothing, because they do not want to look stupid. And if they pay, they make an effort, they work harder . . ."

The Sannyasins were all very enthusiastic about therapy groups, because Bhagwan had advised them to participate in them. His directives put a lot of pressure on Sannyasins who did not have money but who wanted to participate in the groups along with others. The group process made them more vulnerable. The environment, the language, and the expectations—all this made them more prone to exploitation. Everyone wanted to grow, to become meditative, to give up their ego.

In the commune ego was a word to be avoided and detested. Nobody wanted to have anything to do with it, and yet everybody had it. We all tried to hide it. In my opinion all these big words—ego, meditation, and enlightenment—were used to camouflage serious emotions and mask exploitation. Everyone was so crazy for enlightenment and so zealously anxious to be without ego and to be meditative that they could do anything for it. The Sannyasins participated in sexual activities, emptied their pockets, and proved their devotion by expensive gifts and the like. This exploitation was dirty, ugly, and repulsive, especially coming from Bhagwan. He totally exploited His people. But with Bhagwan, it was also possible to learn if one was willing and ready. This exploitation was a price that I gladly paid and paid to the fullest extent.

Soon the groups were running very well. The ashram became known worldwide for Bhagwan's group therapies. He soon transferred the responsibility of booking the groups and recommending groups to the new comers to us. He gave us general guidelines for the distribution of the Sannyasins. The groups for beginners were quite harmless. But the advanced groups were stricter and harder. The harder therapies such as primal groups and encounter groups were offered only to persons who had participated in at least ten other groups, or to people who knew Bhagwan's working methods and trusted them. We only asked for Bhagwan's advice when a participant had medical problems or when there were other difficulties. All therapists worked under His guidance, and He was always informed about what was happening in these groups. In the beginning He gave Teertha complete freedom with his encounter groups until there were negative press reports everywhere about violence and rapes in his group. This publicity was a nightmare for us. After this no journalists were allowed to participate in encounter groups anymore. The therapists were encouraged to be cautious when cameras were nearby. They were encouraged to act more restrained and responsibly and offer no more reasons for any bad publicity. There was also no more violence in the groups. The therapies became more harmless, including the encounter groups.

Bhagwan had the reputation of advocating frequent changes of sexual partners. His famous book *From Sex to Superconsciousness* was thought to be pornographic by many Indians. Their religious feelings were violated because a holy man had spoken so openly about sex in the book and had given sex a religious legitimacy. These ideas were not received well. He became the enemy of all sexually repressed saints and sadhus. On the other hand, this sympathetic attitude of Bhagwan toward sex served many sex-hungry men and women justification for promiscuous behaviour. The apparent freedom to express their feelings was seen as encouragement to frequently change sexual partners.

Bhagwan was also accused of being sexually very free with women around Him in the ashram. According to the commonly accepted standards holy men must not deal with such sensual issues at "lower planes of existence." I can still remember very well how one of my aunts warned me of Bhagwan. She told me, "Be careful when you visit him. Do not go alone into his room with him; you are a young girl."

Because of the press reports about therapy groups and Bhagwan's discourses about sexual matters, He was threatened by violence. Average Indians soon avoided having anything to do with Him. They were very skeptical, afraid and conservative. The hostility against Bhagwan grew.

14
Progress in Poona

When the ashram in Poona became a world-renowned therapy and growth centre, we had to expand quickly and extensively. For both types of Sannyasins—those who had permanently shifted to Poona and those who were mere transient visitors—a better infrastructure was needed. Their personal needs such as shelter, food, clothing, health, and entertainment had to be taken care of.

These necessities were a natural consequence of our growth.

Bhagwan used these needs for the extension of the ashram and its activities. The business activities associated with fulfilling these needs made us immediately self-sufficient.

When Bhagwan was still living in Bombay, there were five people who lived with Him in His apartment and cared for His physical needs. The move to Poona also necessitated an increase in that number because He now lived in a big house. He needed more staff. The organization He had in Bombay was no longer sufficient.

As we were now the most important therapy centre in the

world, we urgently needed to take care of the needs of the therapy group participants as well. In all, there was a lot of work to be done. Many different job-positions needed to be filled. The days of unrestrained leisure and laziness had come to an end.

Laxmi was asked to buy as many parcels of land as possible in the vicinity of Bhagwan's house. She had already bought a second house right behind the first just one month after His move. Bhagwan's house was called Lao-Tzu House. The second house, at the main entrance of the Rajneesh ashram, where the offices were located, had been named Krishna House.

Within a short time, the ashram became a closed area of nearly 25,000 square meters with three main buildings and many other structures, some erected legally with permits and others without legal permits. The illegal structures were built predominantly out of a need to get things done in a timely manner in the face of long delays expected in procuring building permits, delays which could be shortened only by paying numerous bribes. It became a trademark of the Rajneesh movement to not be hindered by legal formalities.

For the purchase of additional land and other necessary renovations, a lot of cash was required. The therapy groups had only just started. The income from the groups was not yet enough to fund everything. Donations from Indian Sannyasins were limited since Bhagwan had not been giving as much attention to them as before. They were angry with Him. He had been mostly focusing on the Sannyasins from the West. The gap between Indians and people from the West was widening. And we, the workers, had to be creative in order to find more money.

One evening Laxmi looked deeply worried. We sat in her office after the day's work was done. She often worked long hours, and we often joined her late in the evening and gossiped with her. Gossip was a major source of entertainment in ashram life. We laughed and talked about all kinds of things.

That evening I asked her why she looked so down. She told me that by the next evening, she had to raise a large sum of money. This amount was part of the price for a house next door, which we wanted to buy for the expansion of the ashram. It was very important. The purchase was urgently needed. I innocently asked her how much money she needed. I then calculated the amount in dollars. It was a large sum, but it was not impossible.

With her approval, I began my work the next morning after the discourse. I stood in front of the gate of the Lao-Tzu House that opened to the auditorium where discourses were held. I asked everyone who came out whether they could lend me money for buying a new building.

I had a notepad with me, on which I took down all the details about the loan: the name of the creditor, the amount, the currency, and when the money had to be paid back. Before lunch, I had more money for Laxmi than she needed. And not only that, she had the money in foreign currency. That meant we had a solid base to negotiate a very favourable loan agreement with the banks, because we would have foreign currency to offer as security. This little incident made me instantly popular with Laxmi.

The system of borrowing money from the Sannyasins became a permanent institution. With this system, I founded the unofficial Ashram Bank. Soon it had a daily turnover of more than a hundred thousand dollars. And there were more than half a million dollars in liquid cash available always.

The theft of their identity cards and traveller's checks was a big problem for the Sannyasins who didn't live in the ashram. The accommodations outside the ashram were not safe. So, we even had to build bank lockers for the valuables of these Sannyasins. Inevitably, as the bank grew bigger, we had to staff it with three full-time workers. In no time, it became a very important source of income for the ashram.

We were aware that setting up the bank without any government permits or licenses was not legal. But we never did anything illegal willfully. We were forced to go against the law since official blessings generally took eternities to come.

We also had to set up a complete healthcare system for our people. Doctors and medicines were an important issue for the Sannyasins and the community. The visitors from the West very often suffered from colds and diarrhoea, being unaccustomed to the Indian air, water and food. Infections were almost a permanent condition. And the local doctors did not meet the desired standards common in the West. So we built our own medical centre with a wide range of doctors and nurses from many different countries. The result was a modern facility, multilingual like the rest of the commune. This medical centre was built near the ashram's main building for everyone's convenience. It was well equipped according to Western standards; a clean, functional space.

For the ashram residents and full-time workers, the medical assistance was free of charge. The others paid a monthly amount, almost like an insurance premium. We also had a pay-for-service option. The money from this healthcare system was used for its further expansion and also to set up a dental facility.

Later a school for the children was also needed. In the beginning, the people who came to Bhagwan were mostly young, single hippie types without families, who were travelling through India in search of spiritual teachings. Later the somewhat better-off professionals also began to come, and finally whole families began arriving. In the ashram there were strict rules regarding children. Bhagwan did not want children in the limited space we had. So He would not only discourage young female Sannyasins from becoming pregnant, He also encouraged abortions and sterilizations.

Bhagwan had asked many workers of the ashram who held important positions to be sterilized, because pregnancies and children could become a problem for them. Bhagwan argued that the world was already heavily burdened with unwanted children and to produce more of them was criminal. The ashram had a clear attitude toward pregnancies. Neither did births take place inside the ashram, nor were pregnant women allowed to live inside.

Eventually, the press came to know about these directives against childbirths. This added to His growing infamy. Shortly after the press sensationalized the issue, it was decided that the time had come to provide for the care of children in the commune. But the shortage of space was a big problem, and to encourage large families to come before sufficient space was available for them was not appropriate.

Relief came when some of the early families decided to set up their own kindergartens in their homes outside the ashram and allowed children of other Sannyasins to attend them as well. Bhagwan used this opportunity to give young mothers moral support by talking about issues related to children and their needs. He advised Laxmi to not be involved directly with the kindergartens outside the ashram, but to just keep an eye on them.

There were some people among these families who were doing really good work in the ashram. In order for these people to continue their work at the ashram without any difficulty, Laxmi persuaded Bhagwan to declare the kindergartens a part of the ashram. This move had an extra advantage: the additional space attached to these kindergartens could be used as accommodations, which we so desperately needed for the workers. Once the ashram was actively involved in the kindergartens, Bhagwan gave them a name: Ko Hsuan (after a famous Zen master). Later a full-fledged school emerged from it. It developed into an important part of the commune. He told us how the school should be run:

The commune of my vision will have a five-dimensional education. Before I enter into those five dimensions, a few things have to be noted. One: there should not be any kind of examination as part of education, but every day, every hour observation by the teachers; their remarks throughout the year will decide whether you move further or you remain a little longer in the same class. Nobody fails, nobody passes — it is just that a few people are speedy and a few people are a little bit slower — because the idea of failure creates a deep wound of inferiority, and the idea of being successful also creates a different kind of disease, that of superiority.

Nobody is inferior, and nobody is superior.

One is just oneself, incomparable.

So, examinations will not have any place. That will change the whole

174

perspective from the future to the present. What you are doing right this moment will be decisive, not five multiple-choice questions at the end of two years. Of thousands of things you will pass through during these two years, each will be decisive; so the education will not be goal-oriented.

In the past, the teacher has been of immense importance, because he knew he had passed all the examinations, he had accumulated knowledge. But the situation has changed — and this is one of the problems, that situations change but our responses remain the old ones. Now the knowledge explosion is so vast, so tremendous, and so speedy, that you cannot write a big book on any scientific subject, because by the time the book is complete, it will be out of date; new facts, new discoveries will have made it irrelevant. So now science has to depend on articles, on periodicals, not on books.

The teacher was educated thirty years earlier. In thirty years everything has changed, and he goes on repeating what he was taught. He is out of date, and he is making his students out of date. So in my vision the teacher has no place. Instead of teachers there will be guides, and the difference has to be understood: the guide will tell you where, in the library, to find the latest information on the subject.

And teaching should not be done in the old-fashioned way, because television can do it in a far better way, can bring the latest information without any problems. The teacher has to appeal to your ears; television appeals directly to your eyes; and the impact is far greater, because the eyes absorb eighty percent of your life situations — they are the most alive part.

If you can see something there is no need to memorize it; but if you listen to something you have to memorize it. Almost ninety-eight percent of education can be delivered through television, and the questions that students will ask can be answered by computers. The teacher should be only a guide to show you the right channel, to show you how to use the computer, how to find the latest book. His function will be totally different. He is not imparting knowledge, he is just making you aware of the contemporary knowledge, of the latest knowledge. He is only a guide.

With these considerations, I divide education into five dimensions. The first is informative, like history, geography, and many other subjects that can be dealt with by television and computer together. The second part should be sciences. They can be imparted by television and computer too, but they are more complicated, and the human guide will be more necessary.

The first dimension also includes languages. Every person in the world should know at least two languages; one is his mother tongue, and the other is English as an international vehicle for communication. They can also be taught more accurately by television – the accent, the grammar, everything can be taught more correctly than by human beings.

We can create in the world an atmosphere of brotherhood: language connects people and language disconnects too. There is right now no international language. This is due to our prejudices. English is perfectly capable, because it is known by more people around the world on a wider scale – although it is not the first language. The first is Spanish, as far as population is concerned. But its population is concentrated; it is not spread all over the world. The second is Chinese; that is even more concentrated, only in China. As far as numbers go, these languages are spoken by more people, but the question is not of numbers, the question is of spread.

English is the most widespread language, and people should drop their prejudices – they should look at the reality. There have been many efforts to create languages to avoid the prejudices – the Spanish people can say their language should be the international language because it is spoken by more people than almost any other language.... To avoid these prejudices, languages like Esperanto have been created. But no created language has been able to function. There are a few things which grow, which cannot be created; a language is a growth of thousands of years. Esperanto looks so artificial that all those efforts have failed.

But it is absolutely necessary to create two languages – first, the mother tongue, because there are feelings and nuances that you can say only in the mother tongue. One of my professors, S. K. Saxena, a world traveler who has been a professor of philosophy in many countries, used to say that in a foreign language you can do everything, but when it comes to a fight or to love, you feel that you are not being true and sincere to your feelings. So for your feelings and for your sincerity, your mother tongue... which you imbibe with the milk of the mother, which becomes part of your blood and bones and marrow. But that is not enough – that creates small groups of people and makes others strangers.

One international language is absolutely necessary as a basis for one world, for one humanity. So two languages should be absolutely necessary for everybody. That will come in the first dimension.

The second is the enquiry of scientific subjects, which is tremendously important because it is half of reality, the outside reality. And the third will be what is missing in present-day education, the art of living. People have taken it for granted that they know what love is. They don't know... and by the time they know, it is too late. Every child should be helped to transform his anger, hatred, jealousy, into love.

An important part of the third dimension should also be sense of humor. Our so-called education makes people sad and serious. And if one third of your life is wasted in a university in being sad and serious, it becomes ingrained; you forget the language of laughter – and the man who forgets the language of laughter has forgotten much of life.

So love, laughter, and an acquaintance with life and its wonders, its mysteries... these birds singing in the trees should not go unheard. The trees and the flowers and the stars should have a connection with your heart. The sunrise and the sunset will not be just outside things – they should be something inner, too. A reverence for life should be the foundation of the third dimension.

People are so irreverent to life.

They still go on killing animals to eat — they call it game; and if the animal eats them — then they call it calamity. Strange... in a game both parties should be given equal opportunity. The animals are without weapons and you have machine guns or arrows... You may not have thought about why arrows and machine guns were invented: so that you can kill the animal from a faraway distance; to come close is dangerous. What kind of game is this? And the poor animal, defenseless against your bullets.

A great reverence for life should be taught, because life is God and there is no other God than life itself, and joy, laughter, a sense of humor — in short a dancing spirit.

The fourth dimension should be of art and creativity: painting, music, craftsmanship, pottery — anything that is creative. All areas of creativity should be allowed; the students can choose. There should be only a few things compulsory — for example an international language should be compulsory; a certain capacity to earn your livelihood should be compulsory; a certain creative art should be compulsory. You can choose through the whole rainbow of creative arts, because unless a man learns how to create, he never becomes a part of existence, which is constantly creating. By being creative one becomes divine; creativity is the only prayer.

And the fifth dimension should be the art of dying. In this fifth dimension will be all the meditations, so that you can know there is no death, so that you can become aware of an eternal life inside you. This should be absolutely essential, because everybody has to die; nobody can avoid it. And under the big umbrella of meditation, you can be introduced to Zen, to Tao, to Yoga, to Hassidism, to all kinds and all possibilities that have existed, but which education has not taken any care of. In this fifth dimension, you should also be made aware of the martial arts like aikido, jujitsu, judo – the art of self-defense without weapons – and not only self-defense, but simultaneously a meditation too.

The new commune will have a full education, a whole education. All that is essential should be compulsory, and all that is nonessential should be optional. One can choose from the options, which will be many. And once the basics are fulfilled, then you have to learn something you enjoy; music, dance, painting – you have to know something to go inwards, to know yourself. And all this can be done very easily without any difficulty.

I have been a professor myself and I resigned from the university with a note saying: This is not education, this is sheer stupidity; you are not teaching anything significant.

(Osho, *Golden Future, chapter #23*)

Within our first two years in Poona, the number of Sannyasins increased to 2500. Approximately 1000 of them lived on the premises purchased or rented by the ashram. The remaining 1500 had to find their own accommodations, though even these Sannyasins took their meals in the ashram and spent almost their entire time there. The Sannyasins who lived and worked in the ashram did not pay for their food and room. We all shared rooms and slept in shifts since space was so limited. A restaurant called Vrindavan catered to visitors. It was a paid service. It was clean and served good food.

The basic areas of work were cooking, cleaning, shopping, and gardening. Then there was a large department that worked on the publication of Bhagwan's books. It included designers, proofreaders, printers, and layout experts. Next there was the press department that dealt with publicity and media. There were also multi-lingual guides who led visitors through the ashram.

We had hundreds of typists and accountants, and also handymen for all sorts of repairs. There were carpenters, metalworkers, security people, booksellers, teachers, drivers, doctors, medical staff, and many, many other professionals. There was even a theatre group that used to perform Shakespeare in many big cities of India. We were also proud of our fashion products. There were regular fashion shows in the ashram. Lastly, to make music, which was a part of our daily life, we had fully equipped audio studios as well. Whatever you can imagine, we had it there.

All in all, we had created a fully functioning, multi-dimensional society in the ashram. It was like an independent city in the middle of Poona. We cared for the needs of our people. Everything we did, we did it as best as possible. The quality of our work was excellent. We did it out of love for Bhagwan or as a part of meditation, not for financial reasons. Love and surrender were the basis of our work.

The gates of the ashram opened at six o'clock in the morning for Dynamic Meditation. At this time our workday also started. For the visitors the day in the ashram ended with the last meditation at nine o'clock in the evening. Many Sannyasins preferred work to meditation. During the last two years of our stay in Poona, there was so much to do that we did double and triple shifts in order to cope with existing demands. From early morning until late at night, the ashram hummed like a beehive from all our activities.

Everything has a good and a bad side. Our capitalist lifestyle was sharply criticized. We were known to be materialistic. In the popular mind, spirituality and materialism exclude each other. Many people had one big problem: How could a spiritual master ask for entrance fees for his lectures?

True spiritual leaders are not expected to lead a luxurious life. Spirituality in popular consciousness means material poverty. But Bhagwan had no problem being the guru of the rich. He, in fact, carried this game to its very limit. His lifestyle drove many traditional religious people crazy. His success made them jealous. Many controversies arose, which He liked and which He used to His advantage. To be called materialistic didn't affect Him. He even said once about materialism: *I am not against materialism, because I know that only at the highest peak of materialism does religion happen.*

15
From hypnotic discourses to Bhagwan's silence

It was difficult to characterize Bhagwan. He was everything and nothing. He had the potential of the whole humankind in Himself. He could become both Jesus and Rasputin. When He spoke about Krishna, He was Krishna. When He talked about Mahavir, He became Mahavir. He wore Buddha's diamonds while He lectured on the Diamond Sutra and He became a butterfly with Chuang Tzu. And one could almost see the Zen-stick in His hand when He talked about Zen.

Bhagwan had the goddess of knowledge in His tongue. He spoke fluently in His discourses. He had a captivating melodious voice; He mesmerized and hypnotized. It was a divine experience to hear Him speak. But it was also dangerous. One could very easily become dependent on His words. It was easy to forget oneself in His enticing, flowing words. One could easily lose oneself in them. Often, people would even forget the purpose of their journey once they started listening to Him. For them, hearing Him became an end in itself. It was difficult, almost impossible, to leave His discourses.

I had the feeling that while His words were certainly

important for us, they were also important for Him and His well-being. I had understood very early that His discourses were connected to His health in the same way His life, His work, and His people all depended on His discourses.

One evening, out of the blue, He said to me, "I will no longer speak in public, I am now going into silence." He had hinted at this earlier: "When I would not be able to continue my work, when it would become a burden, then my departure from this earth would be imminent, and I would stop talking."

So when He announced His intentions that evening, I could not believe my ears. I broke into tears. It meant the end of the man I loved. I could not understand why He was doing it. I could only see that His health was not good. I immediately thought: He is going to die soon, and if He stops talking His body would not survive anyway. Talking meant His health.

I felt very responsible for His well-being. Just a few weeks before this event, I had gone to Him for some work. I had noticed that He had to lie down because He was experiencing serious back pain. And these pain attacks came when He coughed a lot because of His asthma. It immensely hurt me to see how He suffered from all this.

And now this—the vow of silence! I said, "A few weeks ago, you had stopped reading and now you want to stop talking?" For years, we had spent thousands of dollars on His books, which Sannyasins brought from the West. He had an impressive library, both in terms of quality and quantity.

He knew what I was feeling and thinking. He said softly, "Seela, do not worry. It is true, my eyes are not so good. From reading I get headaches. I do not want to wear glasses. It was easy for me to stop reading because I have read so much in my life."

Then He continued, "Do not be sad, Seela. You have to be strong. You pass this message to all the Sannyasins. I have worked hard to bring them to this point where they can sit and understand me without any exchange of words. The time has come. From now on I will no longer talk to them. We will communicate in silence. Seela, my silence will assist the work. If I speak, it will only be an obstacle to the work of building the new commune. My silence is necessary to build the new commune. Seela, stop crying and worrying. If you are sad, then the whole ashram becomes sad. If you are sad, then you would not be able to build my new commune."

How true. My feelings were really reflected in Bhagwan's people. When I was happy, then the whole commune was happy. When I was sick or sad, then the whole commune was sad. I could not show my tears in public. For the commune, I had to be always conscious of my conduct.

I was sure that all Sannyasins would feel exactly the same sadness as I did. In my mind, I went over it again and again on how to pass on the news of His vow of silence so that it did not cause as much grief to His people as it had caused me. I was very worried. I called a meeting of the heads of all the departments. These were at least 450 people. To my surprise, most of them accepted the message joyfully.

Whether I was good at passing on the message or whether His people were happy that they would now be in a position to communicate with Him in silence, I don't know. But one thing was sure: they did not feel the same as I did. My concern for His health was very real. I had always enjoyed His words.

They were music to my ears. His voice had a calming effect on me. I was going to miss His discourses. I was going to miss the beauty of His work.

16
Housefull

The ashram in Poona grew steadily. Bhagwan was by now known worldwide. Every day, thousands of visitors came to us. Everything in Poona became hopelessly overcrowded. There were people in orange everywhere. Securing accommodations for this crowd became a major problem. Soon, newly arrived visitors to the ashram had no place to stay.

Everything had become very expensive too. The local businessmen had started exploiting our visitors. To find decent apartments at reasonable prices had become impossible. Bhagwan was aware of this situation. He asked Laxmi to buy all available houses in Koregaon Park, the district in Poona where the ashram was located. But the time was not favourable for land purchases, certainly not in the situation we were in. Firstly, everybody knew that we urgently needed more space. Secondly, everyone believed that the ashram and Bhagwan were very rich. His people were judged to be in a position to pay any price.

Also, the town's businessmen were no longer interested in their usual local customers. They were mainly interested in the foreign Sannyasins who could pay very high prices. The increased prices for common necessities made us the enemies of the local population. Some of them began to search for like-minded people to plan and drive us away from Poona. Orthodox Hindus of the community also offered their support to the activities designed to drive us away.

The Sannyasins soon had to work and sleep in shifts. They would gratefully accept any accommodation, no matter how bad. As long as they could be close to Bhagwan, they were happy with anything. But many of them became ill. The usual feverish colds and infections were also constantly around. Everything was unhealthy. Hygiene was poor. Bhagwan constantly talked against sexual repression and so the Sannyasins lived their sexuality quite freely. As a consequence, STDs became a big problem in our commune. And tracing the sexual contacts of the infected Sannyasins was an impossible task. Some Sannyasins actually had ninety different sexual contacts in a month. I wondered where, after a busy working day, they found the time and energy for so much sex. I asked one of them. He laughingly told me that he had three different contacts per day: one in the morning before breakfast, one after lunch and one in the evening after dinner. I jokingly remarked, "So you have a dessert after every meal . . ."

The dirty accommodations contributed to the overall filthiness. Our hospital soon ran out of beds, and we had no space for expansion. The lack of space and resulting congestion also had a negative impact on the beauty of the ashram.

To make matters worse, Bhagwan became sick again. Allergies, asthma, back pain and frequent death threats had been forcing Him to stay in His room. And His diabetes made everything as bad as possible. He became a sick man. He stopped His daily discourses. He was not happy. It was time to move on and start something new.

We made the greatest efforts to protect Bhagwan and His health. Since Bhagwan was extremely allergic to perfumes and scents, we had to take extreme measures to eliminate these from coming near Him. Before the morning discourses and evening darshans, each participant was checked for odours and perfumes. For this task certain individuals were designated as "sniffers." They sniffed everybody who wanted to enter Buddha Hall to attend His discourses or darshans. This was a strange ritual, but it was necessary and important. It was meant solely to protect Bhagwan's health and to prevent a severe asthmatic attack.

Bhagwan's provocative lectures had made Him the target of fanatics as well. His security was a major cause of anxiety for us. He had to be always protected. In the early days, when He was still a travelling philosopher, He used to allow people to touch Him. But sometimes visitors would pretend to want to touch His folded hands but then would injure Him with razor blades or needles. We would find out about this only on seeing blood on His hands and handkerchief. So it became essential for us to prevent the audience from coming close to Him and touching Him. We had to take many precautionary measures. This was no paranoia. The threats were quite real.

I personally witnessed two attacks on Him, one in Bombay and one in Poona. Even now I can remember them clearly. One was during an evening discourse in Bombay. Bhagwan's words were mesmerizing as usual. We were totally absorbed. After He had talked for half an hour, there was a sudden restlessness in the crowd. An angry drunk man was trying to enter the room. He had an open knife in his hand, and murder was writ on his face. He was very angry at Bhagwan and wanted to kill Him. He was a fanatic. The guards outside the gates were holding him to keep him from entering the room. The unrest soon changed into a fight. Bhagwan stopped talking. He looked at the door and called Narendra, a long-time Sannyasin. He was a cousin of Bhagwan and had been living with Him for many years.

Bhagwan ordered, "Naren, release him! Let him come in."

Narendra did not want to do that. He did not order the release of the man.

Bhagwan strictly commanded him, "Naren, release him! I am telling you, you should let him come in."

Now Narendra had to release him. I could not believe my eyes. From my seat close to Bhagwan I could clearly see the whole scene. The drunk was a madman, extremely dangerous. He was boiling inside and had foam in his mouth. Full of compassion, Bhagwan said, "Come. Come here."

The man went up to Bhagwan, fell at His feet, and cried. Bhagwan put His hand on his head and continued His discourse, as if nothing had happened. He was as fluent as before. There was no interruption. The way He resumed was really remarkable. How can one be not affected by such a situation? For me this was unbelievable.

Later, there was a similar attack in Poona. A man approached Bhagwan and threw a knife at Him, which fortunately missed Him. But He did not even blink His eyes. He did not show the slightest interest in the knife or the man who had thrown it. He did not even turn to see where the knife had come down. He did not stop His lecture even for a fraction of a second.

As a result of these attacks we had to organize stringent security around Bhagwan and had to set up a unit of Sannyasins as bodyguards for Him. They were given the name "Samurais."

For now let it suffice that His delicate health, overcrowding in the ashram, and growing clashes with the orthodox Hindus ultimately led to His decision to move out from Poona.

17
In search of a new land

The year 1980 was difficult for me. This was the year I lost Chinmaya to cancer. His last years were tough. He was confined to bed in our room in the ashram. We lived together in Poona till his end. He did not want to be away from Bhagwan and me. When he died, Bhagwan's teachings gave me the strength to accept the loss.

Chinmaya and I had always been very open with each other. We never slept before sharing our feelings honestly. Though both of us had other lovers from time to time, our loyalty and togetherness never suffered because of it. Our room had a thin partition, so we could entertain our friends when they visited. However, we did have our small and sweet fits of jealousy at times. For instance, once when I saw Gopa's (his then girlfriend) underpants on our beautiful leather chair—which I'd gifted to him on his birthday—I screamed and said, "Next time I see her, she will have a problem with me." And sometimes if someone was visiting me for the night, he would say, "Is your dumb friend coming to visit you tonight?"

Our love was true and pure. I always felt connected to him. I could feel him even if we were thousands of kilometers away. Once I was in New York, and he was in the Poona Ashram. I felt uneasy in the middle of the night. I was restless. I called to check on Chinmaya. Laxmi informed me that they had moved him to a hospital in emergency earlier that night itself. I immediately realized why I was feeling restless.

Whenever I returned from my travels, I would see Chinmaya waiting for me outside our room, as he could not come to the ashram gate to receive me. Chinmaya missed his mother a lot, even though they often spoke on phone. Once, his sister even came to visit us in the ashram. She too became a Sannyasin. I am in touch with her even today.

After Chinmaya's death, I devoted myself to Bhagwan and the ashram completely and even more dedicatedly.

Bhagwan wanted a new site where we could build the commune of His dream: a community in which thousands of people could live together harmoniously. He wanted to create a Buddha field—an energy field that could provide for all the people who wanted to live and meditate together in a friendly, loving environment. It was supposed to be a space where one could complement the weaknesses of others with one's own strengths.

His secretary Laxmi tried to find a suitable site in India. But the political situation was very unfavourable. Under the government of the then prime minister Indira Gandhi, and later under Morarji Desai, emergency laws were put in force. These included the prohibition of all land sales. Prime Minister Morarji Desai, who was very orthodox and conservative in his views, was a self-proclaimed enemy of Bhagwan, because Bhagwan had often made fun of his politics, his intelligence, and of his odd personal habit of drinking his own urine for medicinal value. Also since the masses never understood Bhagwan's message, it was dangerous for any politician or a government official to be connected with Him. The orthodox masses were always afraid of Bhagwan and His message of freedom from all forms of social conditioning.

Under these circumstances, it was difficult to buy land in India. Bhagwan's press policy made this project even more difficult. He was constantly pouring new oil into the fire by generating controversies through His ideas. This led to even more hostility towards Him in public. And it also undermined Laxmi's efforts to find a new plot of land. Bhagwan was becoming increasingly impatient and did not want to know or deal with these difficulties any more. He just wanted the problem to be solved. His mood became worse every day. He did not want to live in the stagnant, suffocating ashram any longer. He wanted to move out right away.

So, suddenly, one day in 1980, He declared His secretary Laxmi incompetent and fired her. In His eyes she was a failure since she had failed to find a new location for the commune.

Laxmi was sent to Kutch and Delhi to arrange the land for the new commune and solve the problem of taxes. She was ordered not to return empty handed. He was being unreasonably hard. He knew this task was impossible for her. I too was travelling with Laxmi. Suddenly I was summoned back to see Him and, a short time later, He appointed me as His new secretary, a job that I did not want. I did not consider myself capable of this important position. I was not trained for it.

But Bhagwan was sure.

You can just see Sheela: she is so beautiful. Do you think anything more is needed?

I have chosen her as my secretary because she has lived with me for many years, and I have seen not only her physical beauty, but also her spiritual beauty. I have seen her intelligence. I have seen that she can manage this whole commune of crazy people.

(From "The Fruits Are Ripe," in *Osho: The Last Testament, Vol 1*)

My only strength was my love for Him. Another qualification was my willingness to learn. He did not give me any choice in this matter. I had to simply accept, to trust, and to work. I told myself constantly: if He thinks that I am capable of it, then that must probably be the case. Otherwise He would not have offered the job to me.

He told me work is meditation. I already enjoyed working for Him. And to be able to work with Him more closely— perhaps as closely as possible—was an opportunity one was offered only once in a lifetime, if at all.

For me it was very natural to say yes, because I was full of love and trust. I could not say no to Bhagwan. Fear of failure had no room to enter. It automatically became a yes by itself. I trusted Him profoundly.

It is easy to say yes if one is rooted in one's heart. In the mind everything begins and ends with fear and, therefore, a big no. I was lucky: saying yes was always totally natural for me. Later it was always this Yes, and my love and trust for Bhagwan, from which I got the confidence in myself for my work. From this Yes I got the intelligence to work. I got enough energy from it to work day and night, and night and day, such that time and space became unimportant for me. The only thing that mattered was Bhagwan and His work. This gave me a clear focus. It let me work with tremendous concentration. Half the battle of work was already won by being so focused.

Even in times when my health was poor, I would be in a position to get up and continue my work, because I had this certainty that I could continue to work as long as the fire of love burnt within me. My body would not fail. The Yes in me overcame every disease. I was aware of the strength of my love. It convinced me. Through my Yes, I saw the potential of the same Yes in other Sannyasins. It was my job to bring forth this devotion and hard work in other Sannyasins under His guidance. To be able to do this, I had to learn to understand the Yes and the No fully. It was easy for me to understand the Yes, because I had experienced it myself.

Bhagwan had explained to me that No is an ordinary experience in the world. The No supports the Ego. Without Ego, No is not possible. The frequency of its use makes the ability to say no a quality that everyone desires.

However, Bhagwan distinguished between a positive and a negative No. A positive No comes from the same space as the Yes. It is the No of the mother who wants to save her child from an accident. It was this positive No and the absolute Yes that lighted my path as Bhagwan's secretary.

For me, India was not a good choice to expand. Everything was slow in India. Most of the workers in the ashram were Westerners. They were all highly qualified, and many had left jobs in high positions to work in the ashram. These people were used to high-quality equipment, like good typewriters; word processors; fine quality recording machines; good copy machines; high-resolution photo equipment; music studios; wood-carving machines; kitchen, restaurant, and baking equipment; dental and medical equipment; etc. Everything that was available in Europe and America, Bhagwan wanted it here in Poona. The quality of the equipment in India was bad, as was the quality of work. Almost all the equipment of the ashram was imported and India had strict import rules. The import tax was very high—200 percent on most goods. To bring even the smallest parts into the ashram was a huge headache, a legal and bureaucratic battle. Especially with Bhagwan's appetite for the good things in life, importing goods became a daily nightmare. And Bhagwan was not the only person for whom we had to import things.

We had to be very creative to stretch the law a bit. I can remember that I spent days and weeks with airport customs officials. I hated the dirt and sweat of Bombay. I could not stand the underpaid Indian customs officials always on the lookout for a reward, a bribe. In no way did I want to bribe someone with money, because such an act would have thrown a bad light on Bhagwan and His ashram. We really did not need more scandals. Just charm and exaggerated compliments were sufficient for this task. Even though I detested doing it I had to entertain the officials. So I went for lunch or dinner with them in the luxurious restaurants of Bombay. I did not mind the part with the food, but to sit with them and talk about meaningless subjects was not easy for me. Often I had to stay in Bombay for days, away from Bhagwan and Chinmaya. The only thing that made me happy was the thought that I was serving His work, His ashram. It was the most terrible job. I could only do it because it was for Bhagwan.

I, who had been pampered by the luxury of the West, found everything in India annoying, frustrating. I liked Western conveniences and Western food. I had brought everything for my personal needs from the United States. With the contents of my suitcase I could have opened a small supermarket. It contained everything from Heinz tomato ketchup to tampons. I had had enough of the dirt and the heat of India. Actually this was the case with the majority of Sannyasins. We used to spend many evenings together singing and exchanging nostalgic feelings about the US.

I had often advised Laxmi to get Him out of India. So, when I had the opportunity, I suggested to Him that we move the ashram to the US, and He agreed. I had the feeling that life would be simpler for all of us in the US. How little did I know at that time! I thought the US Constitution would show more tolerance towards a new lifestyle. Unfortunately, it turned out exactly the opposite. I had thoroughly overestimated the American public, their laws, and their politicians. I was naive. I did not realize how valuable was the luxury of tolerance we had in the crowded and dirty India. I also had no idea what it was like to move a man like Bhagwan from one place to another. As it turned out, it was the most difficult task.

Laxmi remained out of station, either trying to win government approval on the taxes in Delhi or looking for land in Kutch or near Poona. I was ordered by Bhagwan to not inform Laxmi about our plans to move to the US. When I would express my desire to inform her or was concerned for her, Bhagwan would say, "Seela, you concentrate on moving to the US. You have six week. Longer I do not have . . . I will take care of Laxmi. She will join us after we have moved there." And she did, five to six months later.

The news of relocation was suddenly in the air, but to where, no one knew. Speculation was rampant. A troubled time began for the Sannyasins. Nobody knew what was going to happen. The future was uncertain. Even though they worked overtime to be in the here and now, their uncertain future made them nervous and anxious. Distractions were necessary to help them remain calm and focused, so that they could continue to function effectively. Fears and hopes had to be kept under control. To interpret everything that happened close to Bhagwan and to gossip about it became a favourite pastime of the Sannyasins.

I was young. I had a lot of energy, but very little experience. Until now, I had always followed the instructions of Bhagwan. Now I suddenly had to give instructions myself. My management team and I had to plan everything very carefully. This required deep understanding and absolute discretion.

It was a complex task–not simply divided into black and white. It had many colours and shades. From the first to the last step, everything had to remain secret, and it was not easy to keep a secret in our gossip-addicted community. It required a great effort to constantly communicate to all assistants that they maintain silence and work with the awareness of the danger. We did not have the luxury to make mistakes. This was our most important project.

At the same time Bhagwan continued to make crazy demands, which came on top of our other tasks. But we did not mind this. We fulfilled all His crazy wishes joyfully. We saw them as our stairs to growth. At the time, we found His madness amusing as we were full of love for Him. We could laugh about Him and His absurd ideas. Love was instrumental in all things concerning Bhagwan. Love always came first.

He was not the only one whose wishes we had to meet though. Vivek, the woman who cared for His personal needs, was a much bigger problem. Publically Vivek was Bhagwan's nurse and caretaker. But it was an unspoken understanding that she shared Bhagwan's bed. In His name, she would make impertinent, extravagant demands that angered me. Fortunately Bhagwan had given me very clear instructions on how much exploitation I had to tolerate from her and others. Initially, I did not cope with this nuisance very well. They gave me headaches. It was a very narrow tightrope. But with experience, I could master these nuances without great difficulty.

The challenge of getting a passport for Bhagwan was the first major difficult task. He did not want to travel to any government offices. He had clearly told me that I obtain all the documents without Him having to appear personally. He was right. If He would have gone anywhere, then it would not have been possible to keep the whole move a secret. Bhagwan was very well known throughout India. He could not go out without attracting huge crowds of spectators. Also, His crew always had to come along; otherwise they would become angry. How could they be someone special if they were not seen beside Him in public?

In the end, we succeeded in organizing Bhagwan's passport, visa, and also His journey. Everything worked out successfully at the last minute, though it did not leave us enough time to plan and organize everything really well. Many people—Sannyasins as well as bureaucrats—were involved in the operation. Everyone had his own priorities, tasks, and schedules. Everyone wanted to benefit. And Bhagwan did not have the slightest understanding for the practical aspect of things. He simply wanted that everything that needed to be done was done and that it was done sooner than-as-soon-as-possible. Waiting was not His thing. Bureaucracy made Him angry and irritated. Laws did not exist for Him. He stood above them. To resolve these things was my job. I must say that with some experience, I became an expert at it all.

We were lucky to find people in government administration who loved or respected Bhagwan enough to help us. In the American Embassy there was one such soul. She ensured that everything went smoothly and worked like a charm. She held the process under seal until she had a commitment from the State Department of the United States for His entry. She updated us with all the news every hour, so we were always on top of the situation. She saw the urgency of the situation and reduced all the bureaucratic hurdles and waiting times to zero.

I had met this loving and courageous woman named Rose for the first time in 1972, when Chinmaya and I had begun our stay in Bombay with Bhagwan. She was really a rose. At that time she had advised that we register with the American Embassy. Chinmaya was an American citizen, and I had a permanent residence permit (Green Card) for the United States. Because of Chinmaya's illness, I often had to deal with the embassy to get documents or the like. So I came in close contact with Rose. Again, Existence must have planned it that way. Somehow we both developed mutual respect and interest. Whenever I would go to the embassy, she would invite me into her office and we'd talk about the world and the ashram. She was always interested in any news about us and our activities. I often invited her to do so as well. She never got a chance to visit us before the tragedy of Jonestown.

What happened in Jonestown was such a ghastly event that it shook many Americans to their core. This disturbing movement was founded by a preacher named James Warren Jones, and it ultimately led to the deaths of more than nine hundred people in the middle of a South American jungle on November 18, 1978. It was a horrific act of mass suicide that exposed how someone could hypnotize the masses into taking their lives willingly.

After Jonestown, the American embassies around the world were asked by the State Department to be very watchful of all religious and New Age movements. They were ordered to thoroughly look at all institutions where American citizens could be found. So the American Consulate in Bombay had to officially send somebody to Poona to the ashram to check. Rose came for this visit. I personally showed her through the ashram and entertained her during the visit.

The American Consulate also received many calls from America of worried parents or relatives who wanted to know whether their relatives or loved ones were in any danger of similar tragedy at the Rajneesh Ashram. All these enquiries were forwarded to Rose, and she would forward them to me. I would help her with them as a personal favour. She would be grateful for my help. At that time, I had not known that in the future I would need her assistance to procure a visa for Bhagwan.

She knew that she would be risking her job and her professional career if she helped me get an American visa for

Bhagwan, because she knew exactly how controversial He was. She and I had often talked about Him. Yet she helped me with it. She did not know herself why she took this risk. She was not a disciple of Bhagwan. She had not even met Him personally. She was an Indian born Christian who had no relationship with any ashram or gurus. She could not understand why she felt compelled to help. She only knew that she had to help me.

Without Rose, we would never have been able to obtain this visa. To support her efforts and take some pressure off her, we organized for a fax to be sent from the State Department in Washington, D.C. to the American Embassy in Bombay. It came from a major lobbyist who supported the visa. The fax was signed by the then Secretary of State, Alexander Haig. We had to pay $7,000 to that lobbyist as his legal fees. We had hired this lobbyist for solving our immigration problems.

These American lobbyists are a very special kind of men. They hang out in the large lobbies of the Senate and of the House of Representatives, and wait for opportunities to negotiate with the politicians. Politicians and lobbyists are in league with each other. The lobbyists support the politicians, and the politicians support the interests of these lobbyists.

Besides the visa, there were other issues we had to sort out as well. Every effort of Bhagwan to leave India would have been interpreted as an escape from tax payments. There were taxes levied on the ashram, but not on Bhagwan personally. Bhagwan lived a rich man's life, but He did not have any personal income or His own property. That's why He never had to pay taxes. During the government of Indira Gandhi and Morarji Desai, many emergency laws were put into force for individuals, and also for organizations. All religious institutions and ashrams in India lost their status as non-profit organizations. They were asked to pay back taxes amounting to millions of rupees for donations they had received in the past. Each ashram, each temple, each church was affected. Each institution was facing a legal dispute. They all had to wait patiently until the emergency laws were repealed and the courts began functioning normally again. But despite all this, the headlines would have been: *Bhagwan escapes from tax payments*.

At each level of our plan, we had to proceed cautiously because of this. We could not allow such misunderstandings to arise, because then the resources of the ashram would have been frozen or detained by the authorities. There were no such occurrences though, mainly because Bhagwan personally did not owe any taxes, neither was He running from them. His two main reasons for leaving India were His health and His life task of creating a new commune for a New Man. But we all knew there was no escaping the tax issues. We knew sooner or later Bhagwan would be faced with a legal battle.

Money was another problem. In India the general standard of living was low, and it was easy to redress financial problems. In America, everything was different. Every little thing was expensive. We had to finish the ongoing operations in India and make a new start in America. The former broke the cash flow abruptly and the latter demanded a lot of cash. Without regular income, it was going to be difficult to move the gigantic ashram to America. It was like transporting a functioning and living city with a few thousand inhabitants to another place, and doing it without any regular income. Apart from this, the much larger running costs of the commune in America had also to be covered. And on top of this came the extravagant personal wishes of Bhagwan. For Him, everything had to be the best and the most expensive, and it had to be in abundance. One golden ball pen was not enough. There had to be hundreds—in yellow gold, white gold, platinum; with rubies, emeralds, diamonds. He did not want only one famous brand name, but all of them, from Caran d'Ache to Dupont, from Cartier to Montblanc. Bhagwan's whole approach to money and worldly needs was not normal. But we had learned to live with these demands and sometimes found them funny. Two things saved us: a) our team's efficiency; we were very creative in finding new businesses to earn money, and b) the money inflow from donations and other ashram events.

Another difficult task was transporting about 2,500 ashram members to America. This was a very complex matter. Flight, accommodation, and residence permits were just some of the aspects with which we had to deal.

Bhagwan led me through all these tasks with ease. He told me what I needed to do. How I got the job done was left to me. Bhagwan was my bouncing board—I would often share all the particulars with Him, but sometimes He would get impatient with me for giving Him too many details and say, "Seela, I trust you. You will do it right."

When I asked Him how to announce the move to the Sannyasins, He told me to pass this message to them: "Everyone has to go back to his or her hometown for some time and put my teaching into practice in normal life. Everyone has to live in his old environment in a meditative way. They can come back when the new commune is ready, when they are invited to live with me in a Buddha field . . ."

This communication helped us remove several difficulties

at the same time. However, we could not issue this message before Bhagwan had left India. Any announcement would have led to a feeling of insecurity among the Sannyasins and the residents of Poona. All of them had a lot to lose from Bhagwan's departure.

If the Sannyasins had got to know that Bhagwan was flying to the US, everyone would have wanted to immediately fly with Him. Panic would have been inevitable. Many Sannyasins thought that their enlightenment would be jeopardized if they could not stay within sight of Bhagwan. And the loss of enlightenment was considered fatal by them. This greed for enlightenment was so strong that reason and logic had no place in their life. The so-called meditators—Bhagwan's guests, the gardeners, His car mechanic, and others—behaved the least helpful when moving. Their only interest was to maintain their secure positions, so they could continue to behave as if they were special. They thought of themselves as spiritually advanced souls. They almost floated around the area. Their feet never touched the ground. It was difficult for me to get along with these people. I had no joy in working with them. Their glum faces wore expression of their true spiritual progress. I often thought that if serious, sour faces and apathy towards others are the outcome of spirituality and enlightenment, then I am happy to be far from it all.

I delighted in the company of hard-working people, those who were flexible and understanding and those who had no expectations, who were just happy to be able to work for Bhagwan and His commune, and who were not concerned about whether they were to leave Poona first or last. These workers went on to be the pillars of the new commune. They worked day and night, night and day. They did not complain. They were not interested in securing a seat in the first row during a discourse. They did not want any special recognition by Bhagwan. But when Bhagwan happened to look at them or smile at them, they would simply melt away and dissolve. These were the workers that made the emergence of the new commune possible later.

Bhagwan was glad to leave India. I, Vivek, and some trusted workers left with Him. We had already sent some people before to prepare the place where Bhagwan would be housed until the commune and His dream house were ready. Savita and Vidya remained behind to inform the public and to see that each Sannyasin was helped through their transition. They had a very hard-working and devoted crew of workers. The sannyasins who went to prepare for Bhagwan, who went with Bhagwan and who remained behind, all knew how important it was to make sure that the news that Bhagwan had left did not become public knowledge until He was safe and settled.

All of us took the needed care to keep our mouths shut and not participate in any gossip. All the trusted workers felt privileged to be involved in this very important event of Bhagwan's life. Only Bhagwan and his sannyasins could pull such a stunt.

We had reserved all the first class seats of a Jumbo Jet leaving Bombay. From the beginning to the end, it was a beautiful flight. I was completely enthralled—what a big task! When we arrived at the airport in Bombay, we drove Him directly to the aircraft, so He could embark immediately. It was a long way to His cabin from the rear end of the jet. He said,

"Such a large airplane, Seela?" He had never before seen such a big plane and had never flown before. It was going to be His first flight. I told Him, "It is a 747 Jumbo," and described the aircraft and its capacity.

We had a smooth start. During the flight, two of my long-cherished wishes were fulfilled. For years I had worked as a waitress and had served drinks to thousands of people. I wanted to once serve something to Bhagwan as well. It was my dream to serve Him a glass of champagne or wine. For me, it would have been the greatest honour to be allowed to serve Him. So I asked Him if He would like to drink a glass of champagne. He said, "If you pour it for me, Seela, yes."

With this my first dream came true. He let me bring Him a glass of champagne. My second dream was to be allowed to clean His room and His bathroom, such that everything was clean, beautiful, and perfect for Him. This I could also do on the flight. These were simple things, but I enjoyed them immensely. I loved Him, and these little things had a lot more value for me than being a great meditator.

This flight was an opportunity for me to treat Him as a lover. He had been locked in a room with the same things for a very long time in Poona. So I wanted to show Him some other things that belonged to ordinary life in the flight. This was my chance. I could not miss it. We flew over Frankfurt, Germany. I liked pumpernickel and cheese. So I asked Him, "Bhagwan, have you ever eaten pumpernickel?"

"And what is that, Seela?" was His reply.

I said, "It is a very famous German bread, made from various grains. I love it. It tastes best to me with cheese. Would you like to try something like that?"

To my amazement, He smiled and said, "Why not?"

He ate pumpernickel with strawberry yogurt. He had never eaten either of these before. With each bite He tried, I felt the joy of a mother bird teaching its babies to fly.

One of the most beautiful moments during our flight was when Bhagwan took some sips from a glass of champagne which I had brought Him and then handed the glass to me saying, "Now you have something to drink, Seela." It was more than I could cope with. I overflowed with joy. That was a moment of trust, of the deepest intimacy between us—such an honour, such closeness!

I wanted to share this joy with the others. I took the glass to the other Sannyasins who were flying with us, but who sat in the tourist class, and shared the champagne with them.

When I returned, He asked for a bottle and a glass. He poured me a full glass, gave it to me, and said, "Seela, now I pour wine for you."

I understood Him. It was the moment for which I was born and for which I would have died. Once again, I drowned in the love that I had for Him and which He showed me. I saw stars in broad daylight.

The whole trip was beautiful, and He was really sweet. He did not complain about anything. He even said to me once, "Seela, if you make travelling so easy for me, then I can even travel around the world and visit all the centres!"

The most divine moment was when I offered Him my hand to help Him enter the airplane and go up and down the stairs in the plane. He accepted my hand and held it warmly and firmly, as if there was no power on earth that could separate us. That was it. Nobody could separate us. It was a very deep contact. In this contact everything was included, the worldly and the divine. Even today we are together. He holds my hand, and I hold His. We are supporting each other, and we mutually care for each other.

To serve Him, to care for Him, and to look after His convenience were very special moments for me. Meditation and enlightenment meant nothing to me when compared to these moments.

I would be perpetually drunk from His wine, His wine that He served me with every gesture, every glance, and with every smile. The intoxication of this love gave me the courage to do anything and everything that He asked me to.

When we arrived in the US, we were all excited and tired. The flight had been the result of many days of hard and honest work. We had put all of our energy into it, maybe even more.

But the journey was not yet over. It had only just started.

18
A castle transforms into a meditation centre

We safely landed at the Kennedy Airport and passed the immigration counters without difficulties. My enthusiasm was boundless. I had witnessed a miracle. I had transported Bhagwan—one of the most precious jewels in the world, a man as fragile as a glass statue, and a visionary so valuable that no amount could have been enough to insure Him—in a fitting style to the New World to begin work to build a commune for the New Man.

Before leaving India, there were three major tasks before us. First, to get Bhagwan out of India safely. Second, to find a fitting site somewhere in the US where we could build the new commune of Bhagwan's vision. And, third, to obtain a permanent residence visa permit for Bhagwan so that He could remain in America. We had successfully accomplished the first task. The second and third still remained.

Years ago, when I was studying in Montclair, New Jersey, I had become very fond of it. The city was very pretty. I had met my first love, Chinmaya, here. After joining Bhagwan, I even opened our first meditation centre—Chidvilas Rajneesh Meditation Center—in the same city, as per Bhagwan's wishes. Bhagwan had Himself given us the name for this meditation centre circa 1973. Chinmaya and I lived in New Jersey at the time and travelled back and forth between India and US to earn money and be with Bhagwan.

After Chinmaya and I permanently moved to the Poona Ashram in 1974, the centre was run by Sannyasins who lived in the area. However, I continued to travel to the US at least a couple of times in a year to shop for the ashram. During one of these trips, I managed to register Chidvilas as a non-profit organization to further Bhagwan's teachings and obtained a tax exemption certificate for it. At the time, I did not know how valuable it was going to prove to be in the future. It appeared as if something unfinished would bind me to this city.

At the beginning of our relationship, Chinmaya and I used to often drive around this little city in our car. We had even hunted down a special secluded place where we could park the car and be together. It was a private lot with a castle called Kip's Castle on it. It was located on a hill which offered a beautiful view of the New York skyline. On clear nights the lights of New York appeared as if they were the gates of heaven.

For us this place was paradise. We visited it very often. We would park our car directly in front of the sign "Private Property," which was installed in front of the castle. From there we would go for long walks. We would not disturb anybody, and nobody would bother us. There would be no other cars around, nor any police checks.

In our moments of togetherness, Marc used to sometimes say to me, "If I ever become rich I will buy you this castle,

Pie." Marc always called me "Chocolate Pie." I was deeply in love with him.

After Chinmaya passed away in the Poona Ashram, I had a new lover. He was a Sannyasin from the same area of New Jersey. His name was Swami Jayananda, though he was popular as Jay.

Jay had very clear-cut and firm ideas about how the ashram and Bhagwan should be and how they should act. Initially I found him difficult but, gradually, I began to find him amusing or even funny. After all no one could *seriously* define how Bhagwan should behave. Everyone knew that Bhagwan would never follow someone else's ideas about how to live. Bhagwan could not behave normally. And if *He* was not normal, how could one expect His ashram to conform to someone else's idea of "normal"?

My coming together with Jay happened under strange circumstances. During one of my shopping trips to the US to buy things for the ashram and Bhagwan, I also visited the Chidvilas Center. Sannyasins from the neighbouring areas were gathered there to hear news about Bhagwan and the ashram in Poona. I was known as one of Laxmi's most trusted assistants. Everyone wanted to hear gossip, especially about where the ashram would move to. Jay was also there.

Chinmaya had died just a few months ago. I was still a young, grieving widow. Chinmaya's death was widely known as Bhagwan had spoken a great deal about it. He was the first Sannyasin to die in the Poona Ashram. He was supposed to be reborn as Ko Hsuan, as Bhagwan had declared. Everyone wanted to know whether he had already been reborn. We talked until late into the night. We ate and drank wine together.

The next day I was scheduled to fly back to India. I urgently needed some rest. In the three weeks of my stay in America, I had travelled a lot and had completed work that would have normally taken three months to complete. Therefore, I wanted a little rest. I said good night to the visitors and went into the small room they had prepared for me. I undressed and went to bed. I was almost asleep when the door opened. I thought that someone had entered the room to get something. I did not even bother to open my eyes. I felt someone pushing me to the side towards the wall and laying himself beside me. For a moment I thought that whoever it was did not know that it was me in the bed, and not his lover. But this was not the case. It was Jay, and he knew I was in the bed. He had come because he was in love with me. He wanted to spend the night with me. He had shown a lot of courage; I could not throw him out of my bed.

Jay was in his mid-forties at this time. He was a confirmed bachelor, but not a womanizer. This courageous act was quite unusual for him. He later told me that he had fallen in love with me several years ago when he had seen me for the first time in the ashram on the steps to my office. He had, however, never attracted my attention before this stay in New Jersey. On impulse, the next day he travelled with me to India.

We spent good times together. Bhagwan liked him and had nothing against my friendship with him or with the others to follow. Jay worked closely with me. He was helpful when we looked for land for the commune in Oregon. Later he also tried to bring local politicians and businessmen to our side when hostility began to grow against us. He was a typical American, too fixed in his ideas. We had difficulties with each other because, sometimes, he would be unable to understand properly the need or nature of my work. He did not like how I worked with pressing deadlines all the time. Also Bhagwan had told him on several occasions that he should unquestioningly listen to me where work was concerned. But this was difficult for him. Not only because he was older than me, but also because I was his *wife*.

Jay and I were not married officially. Our wedding was a bizarre affair. It took place in a plane. We were on our way back to Poona, after a trip to the US. I lost a bet with Jay, and the marriage was the result of this loss. Jay did not want to wait till we reached Poona, so he requested the captain to perform the ceremony then and there. Two of our fellow passengers acted as the witnesses.

Later Jay became jealous. While we were together, I had another lover—a Swiss man named Dipo, whom I went on to marry later. Dipo was openly gay. I was the only woman he had ever fallen in love with and perhaps the only one he had had sexual contact with. It was strange for him in the beginning to recognize his feelings for a woman. It was in 1981 that we both realized and declared our interest in one another. Once, he accompanied me on my visits to different centres across Europe.. On our way to Monte Carlo, we expressed our desire to get married to each other. We finally got married on a business trip to Mexico City.

I had worked out a convenient schedule to deal with my two lovers: from lunch until breakfast the next day with Chinmaya, and then from lunch until the next breakfast with Jay, and so on. I had neither the time nor the energy to deal with insecurities and jealousy. But it would be a lie to say that we were beyond such human emotions. From time to time there were fights because of this. Finally, everything ended when I left Rajneeshpuram after resigning from my post in 1985. I asked Jay if he wanted to come with me. He opted to stay with Bhagwan. But Dipo wanted to be with me.

I must say that I spent a wonderful and very enjoyable time with each of my lovers. I loved them very much. And while I was with them, I was as loving and caring as one can possibly be. I had no complaints about them, neither did I accept any complaints from them.

Jay had returned to the US to live in the Chidvilas Rajneesh Meditation Center in Montclair. He had become one of the main workers there. He used to go jogging regularly. On one of these daily runs he met another jogger who turned out to be the owner of the Kip's Castle. He had run into financial problems and wanted to sell the castle.

At that time I was in India. Jay thought that the castle would be a good opportunity to expand the Chidvilas Center. He realized it would also offer more job opportunities to the Sannyasins who lived and worked in the centre. I mentioned all this to Laxmi. She asked me to talk to Bhagwan immediately. Bhagwan understood the advantages that the property offered. I told Him, "I have not seen the castle, but I used to often kiss Chinmaya in front of it when we were studying together. Chinmaya wanted to buy it for me, but he didn't have the money."

Bhagwan smiled and said, "Hmmm. You have kissed Chinmaya there, and he wanted to buy it for you. Tell Jay he should buy the castle for you."

This was the castle I brought Bhagwan to when we first

arrived in America. For me this was a beautiful and memorable event. It seemed as if all my wishes and Chinmaya's wishes and dreams were coming true without our having to do anything about them actively. Chinmaya had always said to me, "Pie, you will some day find a new home for Bhagwan and His people."

There was another coincidence I found the site for the new commune on the anniversary of Chinmaya's death. When this happened, everything—my past, present, and future—seemed to interconnect somehow. In fact, all events in my life seem to serve to either finish some old chapters or balance the account of my life in some way. While sometimes this life account seems to make sense at the moment, when the events take place, but sometimes I feel the picture becomes clear only later. With each event however, a part of the circle gets completed.

19
Big Muddy Ranch, Oregon

Bhagwan had given me a lot of instructions on how He wanted the new commune to be like. In fact, every time He spoke about this topic, the list of His wishes would become longer by a few inches. Even during the flight from Bombay to JFK He added further details.

After it had been decided that we would relocate to America, I was given exactly two months to organize the whole move. This period, however, was suddenly cut short to less than ten days by Bhagwan. It was likewise with the deadline for the search for a new property in the US. He initially gave me six weeks to find a perfect site. But every time I saw Him, He would advance the deadline.

Barely one week had passed when I received a message of disappointment from Him, "Seela, I know that you are unable to find the paradise for which I have been waiting for thirty years."

The fear of failure in me was overpowering. It was not easy to work for Him. He drove me to the brink of madness. Never in my life had I purchased a piece of land or property.

Even during the purchase of the castle in Montclair, I was not directly involved; I had only ordered the purchase. So I had no idea of what all was involved in purchasing real estate. I decided to take the help of my brother Bipin who had been living in the US for many years. Bipin had many contacts, and I knew he would do everything possible to help me. But when I contacted him and gave him all the information—from what the property should look like to how urgently I needed it—he laughed and said, "You cannot do that here, Sheela. It does not work like this in the United States. Here, you have to do this and that and so on. It takes time." Instead of helping me, he gave me his wise advice.

I looked at some properties myself in Tennessee, Colorado, and Arizona in the following days, but they were all disappointing. What I saw was nowhere close to what I had in my mind. From being desperate, I slowly began to feel discouraged. I felt I would never be able to find the land that I had promised Bhagwan.

I again called Bipin and asked him if he knew someone who could help me with my search. Instead of simply answering in yes or no, he had a whole litany of advice ready for me. Then, at last, he said, "I have already organized for someone to come to take you to Oregon. There you can check out a suitable property. It is big and expensive . . ."

The man sent by Bipin picked me up in Arizona where I was checking out other properties. We flew together to Oregon. He told me the price of the property we were going to look at: $7.5 million. I was greatly taken aback.

But when we arrived at the site, I felt quenched. Its air was magical. The freshness of open country and the sunny blue sky completely captivated me. Mount Hood looked beautiful on this clear day. The idea to own that mountain you could see from far away was unbelievable. The entire mountain range and over fifteen kilometres of the John Day River—everything seemed unreal. I fell in love with it at first sight.

For me the most important thing was that I had found something that Bhagwan was sure to like. Most of the requirements on His list could be fulfilled by that piece of land. Not only could Bhagwan have a house there with a beautiful view, but each one of us could have that opportunity there. There were gentle hills on the location and also pretty grazing land with junipers. I also saw a lake, a river, a creek, and also the opportunity to create another lake. A runway for aircrafts was available too. The site was located far from densely populated areas and away from polluted cities. The nearest neighbours lived more than thirty kilometres away in a ghost town called Antelope.

I had found this property within the time frame Bhagwan had given me. It was the sixth day of my search. He had given me one week. It was June 11, 1981, the first death anniversary of Chinmaya. For me, *these* connections were important, and not whether there was enough water or sufficient power supply available at the site, for I always took it for granted that these things would be okay. I told the man that I would like to buy the land.

Jay and Bipin later railed at me for not negotiating the price before openly expressing my feelings. One does not conclude a sale this way. One should initially look disinterested, not simply say, "I like it and I want to buy it." I should have looked disappointed and said, "This is really not what I am looking for." But, alas, I did not know this strategy. I thought that everybody expressed their emotions as openly and freely as I did. I also did not know that there were more important things involved in the process than merely liking the land and paying to buy it. I knew so little.

Jay, who had come with me, took it on himself to investigate the fine print, while I took care of Bhagwan's wishes. Then I started the negotiations. Many questions had to be answered: How would we make the payment? For what purpose we wanted to buy the land? What plans did we have to develop it?

My biggest task was to assure the owners that we could pay and that they need not worry about getting their money. I worked up a detailed payment plan which also included the time when we could take possession of the property and begin to work and live there.

Meanwhile, Bhagwan was constantly forcing me to do everything very quickly. With His deadlines, we did not get the time to even examine the land records and other documents of the site. Neither did we get the time to think over issues such as mineral and water rights that are involved in buying such large properties. Nothing could go fast enough for Him. He had wanted a new commune three years ago. As far as He was concerned, we were already three years late.

Bhagwan's deadlines also made it difficult for us to negotiate the price like clever buyers. It did not matter to Bhagwan how much money was to be paid or whether the price could be negotiated. He simply wanted us to start working on the new commune as soon possible. He had very different priorities. And the dimension from where His demands came was not easy to understand for either an ordinary businessman or for many Sannyasins. But I understood it, and that is why His instructions were more important to me than money. However, my helpers did not sympathize with my attitude. This created friction between them and me. There were conflicts too. Even with Jay I had conflicts, and these were especially hell for me. Sometimes Bhagwan would call and tell him, "Seela is only doing what I tell her. She is not interested in power. She only executes my instructions. You, Jay, have to support and help her; you should not be a problem for her . . ."

But, despite this, conflicts would arise between us. Perhaps, it had something to do with the fact that I was a woman with authority over him, a man, and that, instead of him, I was acting as the representative of Bhagwan and of the commune.

To please Bhagwan, I had to ensure that the property was immediately transferred into our possession. This entailed, however, that we show our cards in that game of poker. The others were not happy about this. They wanted time to be able to check all papers thoroughly. But I could not say yes to this demand of theirs.

So I was accused of not listening to the counsel of people who apparently understood something of worldly affairs. They even advised me to tell Bhagwan that He should keep Himself out of such transactions because He was a spiritual man and did not understand how the world worked. Sometimes I would want to run out screaming and weeping because my very co-workers could not understand that my loyalty was towards Bhagwan and that I could not defy His instructions.

At the end, I succeeded in making everybody accept Bhagwan's and my wishes. And then I agreed to try to negotiate the price.

Even though I did not want to risk losing this property–how could I have gone back to Bhagwan, the man whom I loved, if I were to fail with this business?—I still played my role as an actress during the negotiations later and left the table in the middle of the talks after stating that I could only conclude the contract if my demand to reduce the price to $5.9 million was met. Naturally I told them all the good reasons, which my counsellors had given me, in favour of this discount. After this we came back.

For two days we sat in a hotel room in Bend, Oregon, and had little interest in eating or drinking. Slowly we got on each other's nerves which were ripping tense because of the pressure Bhagwan was exerting on us. It was worse for me because the hurried nature of the negotiations was being mainly blamed on me. My heart hurt very much.

On the second day, I received a call from Vivek. She complained: "Bhagwan knew that you were incapable of finding land for His commune. Now you have brought Him into this foreign country . . ." At this point I clearly told her my opinion. I told her that she should tell Him to look for another secretary.

I could not understand why He reacted like this and conveyed such a message to me when I was already so stressed. Didn't He know the kind of people I was dealing with? I took this very personally. I just put the receiver down, went into the bathroom, and cried. My brother felt that something was not okay. He came up to me and helped me through this situation. Finally, we focused our energies on ending the negotiations. On that very evening, we came to an agreement on all details and concluded the purchase of the Muddy Ranch in Oregon.

I was successful in negotiating the price. We were now saving $1.5 million. Then, without giving any securities, I also acquired a favourable mortgage from the owners. I could thereby spare myself the labourious negotiations with banks and their demands for securities, which I would not have anyway been able to offer. I could have also not shown any guarantees, because I had never done business in the United States.

I was so angry at Bhagwan and Vivek that I did not even call them to tell the good news. The next day we went to Madras, Oregon, signed all the papers, and received all the documents.

The young, inexperienced girl from the small town of Baroda, India, had performed another miracle.

20
Bhagwan's loving surprises

Sometimes I have compared Bhagwan to a master potter. To make pots from clay, one first has to put a lump of clay in the middle of the potter's wheel. Once the mass is correctly centred, the process of forming starts. The clay is supported from the inside and pressure is exerted from the outside. The result: a beautiful pot. This is what Bhagwan did with me. He knew how a loving man behaves. He was charming. He distributed His compliments at the right time in the right way.

I came back from Oregon after completing the purchase of the property. Throughout the entire trip back, I had only one thought on my mind: "How will I ever raise enough money for the first payment?" In ten days I had to pay $250,000 to get the property transferred into our possession. It was no small sum.

I returned late from the journey. Bhagwan had waited up for me. His loving gaze, His hand on my head made me awake again. I fell at His feet. His joyous laughter refreshed my heart. All the fatigue was blown away in an instant. With the greatest interest, He listened to every detail of my story. When I was ready to leave, He held me back with a smile. He said, "Seela, today I saw a car dealer. He was a nice man. He had a beautiful exhibition space. I bought two cars. I told him that my secretary would come tomorrow to pay. Seela, you will do that . . ."

I thought I had not heard it right. I looked at Him again. He was beaming. I laughingly shook my head when I saw Him so. He invited me to accompany Him on a drive the next morning. He wanted to show me His two new cars. I nodded approvingly and left.

I was happy that He had done something by Himself, like a common man. Such a thing had never happened before. It seemed a bit crazy but healthy nonetheless.

Next morning I had a lot of work to do. So I tried to avoid this drive. Not a chance. We got into one of the cars—a Rolls-Royce—and He began to drive.

To drive with Bhagwan, even in a brand new Rolls-Royce, was like giving an open invitation to death. He became a beast behind the wheel. To Him traffic signs were just decorations on the streets. Other drivers used their vehicles for transportation purposes; He rode for fun. As usual, that day too He raced like a madman.

I warned Him, "Bhagwan, there are many maniacs on the road. This is dangerous!"

His answer was, "Seela, there are only two kinds of drivers—the maniacs and the enlightened ones. Do not worry."

When we returned from our trip, He went with me to the second car. It was a bright red Mercedes. He asked me, "Do you like it, Seela?"

When I lovingly nodded, He handed me the keys with a broad smile and said, "I bought it for you! You need a nice car for your work . . ."

He was a man in love. He had come up with this great surprise for *me*. He knew that it had not been easy for me to find a property to fit His requirements. So, as a reward, He had Himself gone to buy a car for me. The mere thought of this was too much for me. He had never done something like this before. At that moment I was not concerned about how I was going to pay for the two cars, let alone the $250,000 for the land. His surprise gift had cheered me up immensely. It flattered my femininity. It was the gift of a lover.

The two new cars amplified the problem of having no money in such a way that now it all started seeming absurd, even funny. Suddenly, all the tension turned into creativity and concerns became laughter. I began to see and feel the problem in a different light. All doors to my inner reserves opened. I remembered Bhagwan's words: Trust. Trust in Existence. One should use money instead of being used by it. Plan the result and put it into action. I called all the workers of the commune together. New priorities were set. We focused on the job in front of us. We begged and borrowed. Money began to flow. While some of it came in the form of donations, some came through loans. The rest came from the sale of our property and our equipment in Poona. There were always timely replenishments. We only had to be creative and clever.

Bhagwan often demonstrated His concern for me with similar loving gestures. This happened months later. I had been working very, very hard. The construction activity in the new commune had reached its peak. We had already held two World Festivals. Bhagwan by then had more than sixty Rolls-Royces, an indication of my success as a fundraiser. I had daily appearances in the media where I was instructed to raise hell for everybody. The intentional controversy program was well under way. Only my health was deteriorating steadily. I was totally overworked and overtired. I could not sleep. My mind was constantly working overtime. My working days were thirty-six hours long.

I was in great pain. My right jaw joint had begun to hurt badly from the constant grinding of my teeth during sleep, courtesy the incredible and incessant stress of building and running the commune and raising funds for it. My jaw joint was apparently overworked and needed to be repaired. I had to have a surgery. Bhagwan did not want me to go to any outside hospital. He believed that I wouldn't be in good hands in a state hospital. So, He ordered an operation room to be built in the commune. He said, "Our medical department can use this room after your surgery. You have always wanted to improve our medical care . . ."

In less than six weeks, everything was ready and equipped for my operation. When I awoke from the anaesthesia in the recovery room, my first thoughts were about Bhagwan. I slowly opened my eyes and asked how He was. I could not believe what I saw. Bhagwan was standing beside me. He smiled at me lovingly and said, "This is not a dream. I am real. I am here. Do not worry about me, Seela, I am fine. Take rest now . . ."

He had come with a carload of colourful roses to visit me.

21
Brick by brick: Building Rajneeshpuram for Bhagwan's arrival

The first work team on the Muddy Ranch consisted of five Sannyasins. These five Sannyasins prepared everything, so that others could follow. To avoid potential public opposition we decided to set up the Oregon commune secretly. We had to shield it from the public, the press, and even our own people. We wanted to get a solid foundation first. It was important that the locals did not begin to react against us out of fear or ignorance. It was also important to prevent any negative publicity about us in the press. In India, due to negative reports in press we had became famous as a sex cult that hosted violent therapy groups, and, as a result, Bhagwan had become a controversial figure both in India and abroad. In the US, moreover, the tragedy of Jonestown was still fresh and vivid in public's mind. Therefore, discretion and confidentiality were crucial for us.

I began to very carefully introduce myself in the neighbourhood. Initially I played the role of a rich, young widow. I pretended to have some ideas about using the dry, over-grazed, and poorly managed land of the ranch for agricultural ends. I explained it mildly as an ecological experiment, a noble project. I offered very superficial details of our plans. And it's not as if whatever I said was misleading. Our plan was indeed to create a vibrant, lively, and thriving commune, which was in harmony with nature. I merely left out details such as the number of people expected to be living there.

At that time, only five people—our first work team which laid the initial foundation for everything that was to follow—were working on the Muddy Ranch. The locals had no problem with this number. They'd expected that at least a few people would come to manage the vast ranch that was almost as big as a city.

The lives of the people in that sparsely populated, isolated region was dull and boring. They were not very receptive to outside influences or ideas different from their own. So it was natural for our arrival to immediately cause a stir among the few farmers in the surrounding area, who led a dusty, forgotten life. They quickly spread a lot of gossip about us. They were curious about what was going on at the ranch.

Meanwhile, it was not easy for us to be unseen. We spoke a different language and dressed differently. In my case, the skin and hair colour were also different. I had very large eyes too. I did not look like an ordinary settler, neither did the others. Even normal settlers are accepted only after several generations. For the locals to immediately accept us would have been unnatural; we knew this.

The rumours about "the money that she has inherited from her late husband" had already made me a subject of hot gossip. We had an aura of mystery surrounding us. I began to behave like a rich, eccentric widow full of charm and intelligence and began to use their imagination to our advantage. Neither was I rich nor was my late husband Chinmaya, but this image helped us obtain necessary credits from the local stores. They all thought I had inherited about $80 million and had put down $7.5 million for the ranch in cash. There was no reason to correct their opinions.

I find it funny that all my life people have projected richness on me, although I neither behave like I have millions in my bank, nor do I dress that way.

We had only one telephone line at the Muddy Ranch and even that was out of commission most of the time. This modern luxury was an absolutely vital necessity for us out there in the middle of wilderness. So we had to think of a solution for this fast. At that time, half of the houses in the town of Antelope were deserted. Many such dead villages existed in Oregon. The young had left to find work elsewhere, while the retired old folks remained there. There was no industry or work possibility in the area. The region was suffering from lack of jobs and opportunity. So we bought a house in the town of Antelope. Here we accommodated our official design office for the ranch. The important thing was that the house had a working phone line. All dealers and suppliers could meet us easily at this house and get instructions on the delivery of goods.

We had no interest in Antelope. For us the ranch was big enough. Our stay in Antelope during the entire period was driven by practical necessities. We were there only to make contact with the outside world until we had built our own infrastructure on the ranch.

We played small tricks to divert attention of the locals. Once I bought myself a pair of cowboy boots and a cowboy hat in a local shop. By doing this, I diverted the attention away from the newly arriving Sannyasins and from other important things such as applying for building permits for fifty houses. Soon, despite our best efforts, people began to notice that strangers were staying in their town and that their number was increasing every day. When this happened, we began to do our daily shopping in the local shops in order to please the shop-owners, even if it meant paying more. They could leave their prejudices aside when it came to doing business. With money one can easily make friends. Not that we were looking for friends, but we certainly could do without enemies.

Next, I carefully began to visit all concerned officials in Jefferson and Wasco counties to share our plans with them. Our property was partly in each of the two counties. While people in Wasco were open towards our arrival, Jefferson behaved more cautiously with us. The people there had a typical small town mentality. They were skeptical and distrustful of newcomers. When the construction of my residence at the ranch was complete, I invited all the responsible officials from Wasco and Jefferson counties to lunch and gave them a tour of the ranch. I had nothing to hide. I thought if they could meet us and see what we were doing, wrong ideas about us would be removed from their heads. Everyone came and remarked positively on our hospitality and openness. Later I even invited the mayor of the town of Antelope to dinner. I wanted them to be friends and not fear us or what we were doing. I was not doing anything wrong or illegal. Friendship and openness have always been my most prized virtues. Even today my house is open to everybody. I am kind to anyone who enters my house, even if it is a Sannyasin!

Once I rented a dance hall and invited all farmers from the surrounding area to a dance party. We served free meals and drinks. This event instantly gave me the reputation of a woman who knew how to throw a good party. More than a hundred people from the neighbourhood came to this dance event. For years there had not been such a party in the locality. It was a huge success. The next morning I had a headache from too much alcohol and sore feet from too much dancing.

I made these social contacts like any good housewife. I knew the importance of putting the neighbours at ease.

During our initial days at the ranch, Bhagwan was not with us. He was at the centre in New Jersey. So during those days I was free to work as I pleased. There was no interference from either Him or Vivek. I enjoyed this freedom very much. Later when I saw Him, I told Him everything down to the smallest detail. He was happy about our progress. But He was interested in only one thing: when was He going to be able to move to the ranch? He described to me exactly how He wanted His house and the ranch to look and everything that should be ready in His house by the time of His arrival. But how were we going to transport His cars and Him there?

I knew that it would be difficult to remove us from the ranch once we had established ourselves there. That was also the case when we had moved to Poona from Bombay. At that time there were many local people who did not want to have Bhagwan and His ashram in their city. Yet, once we had established ourselves, no one was able to remove us from there. Even after Bhagwan left Poona for the US, the ashram remained and still exists.

When we received building permits for the fifty houses we wanted to build, we concentrated on building them as quickly as possible. The simplest solution was to use portable, prefabricated homes. They were cheap and easy to find because this industry was in a slump at this time. We immediately got a model home that had been standing on the parking lot of the company. We set up my office in it so that we could immediately start our work. It was a house with three rooms. For Bhagwan also we bought a prefabricated house. Later, two real structures were built on the area and thereafter expanded in accordance with our needs till they were large buildings with lots of comfort and luxuries. My house, for example, had more than thirty rooms later. There was also a huge living room of about 350 square meters and wide corridors everywhere. Bhagwan's house had a large swimming pool, a well-equipped medical room, a separate room for dental treatment, a recreation room among many others. Later, a new bedroom and living room were also constructed as per His instructions.

When the locals noticed the upcoming fifty homes they started to become suspicious. The Mayor of Antelope began to spread negative rumours about us. Her son had brought her some articles from the German magazine *Stern* in which photos of encounter groups and naked people were printed. She started a written campaign against us. She sent letters to Senator Hatfield and Senator Packwood, two conservative elected Republicans from Oregon. Then she called the *Los Angeles Times* and informed them about our arrival in Oregon.

An *LA Times* reporter soon appeared at my doorstep

without prior notice. Despite this, I welcomed him, showed him the ranch, and answered all his questions. He went back and wrote an article which immediately brought the whole press corps to our doors. Our presence in Oregon was now known to the entire world. It was time for our own announcement, after four months of heavy construction work. We had accomplished a lot during this short period.

The moment *LA Times* broke the news of Bhagwan's arrival in Oregon, the anti-Rajneesh movement started within the local Oregonians. Bhagwan began to be known for His notorious teachings on sex and His controversial encounter groups. His therapies began to be known to the world, and the fear of how Bhagwan and His people might disturb the community and subvert its religion and morals started to take shape. Oregonian politicians saw this as a fertile platform that they could use to their advantage.

Antelope's local population at the time was very minimal. We eventually bought a few houses and converted them into offices and living spaces. But the Sannyasins who had to stay in Antelope were not happy. They felt like outcasts. For most of them, having to live there instead of on the ranch was a punishment.

As a result of the anti-Rajneesh movement, the mayor started causing problems soon. The pressure on the local politicians had also increased. The only option we were left with was to enter the political arena and choose our own citizens to run the government of the county. We eventually won the elections, as the American Rajneeshees were in majority in Antelope. After this legally conducted election we took control of the city council and decided to rename the town of Antelope "City of Rajneesh." It was an intelligent use of the democratic process.

We then decided to make Antelope the entrance to Rajneeshpuram. I have to say that both the praise and the blame must go to the then mayor of Antelope and her anti-Rajneesh friends, because they forced us to take over the city. Certainly they could never have imagined that their anger against us would become the reason for their own defeat. Their anger was a loud invitation to us to get involved with the city and take control of it. Their destructive power was turned against them—like a boomerang.

It was the same with the city of Rajneeshpuram. We only started to think of the possibility of creating our own city when the district authorities, under the pressure of public opinion, refused to provide us with the necessary building permits for more houses. When this happened we had no choice but to take control of the situation into our own hands. We were no politicians. Politics was never our objective. We had to play this game only because we were compelled to do so. Our very existence depended on it. Of course, as it turned out, under Bhagwan's guidance we were really good at it. We were not bound by any preconceived notion of what is right or wrong. We were free souls. Necessity was the basis for our participation in Oregon politics.

Meanwhile more than three hundred Sannyasins had begun to work and live on the ranch to help with the expansion. We worked faster than the difficulties that came towards us. A sense of urgency was in the air. Fortunately, Bhagwan too had moved from New Jersey to the ranch, which we now had named Rajneeshpuram.

This move was expectedly much easier to accomplish than His move from India to America. This time we did not have to worry about passports, visas, or border controls. The greater difficulty had been in containing Bhagwan. He would have preferred to be on the ranch the day we bought it. He was terribly impatient. Like a small child, He would constantly ask, "When can we go? Is the house finished already?"

One morning, a few weeks after the purchase of the ranch, He told me, "Seela, ensure that my house is completed as soon as possible. I would like to be gone from here in two days . . ." None of my practical arguments could change His mind. Once He was determined to do something, nothing could stop Him. I immediately called the ranch and spoke with my trusted friend, colleague, and fellow Sannyasin Padma, who had a great sense of humour and a big heart. She was responsible for building the house and managing the workers in my absence.

"Guess what's new! We come day after tomorrow! Can you have the house ready by then?" First she thought that this was a joke. But once she understood that I was serious, she started to cry. She said it was impossible. The house had only been put in its place two days ago. The foundation had to be finished and all the utilities such as water, electricity, and sewage had to be connected. Landscaping needed to be put in place. And then the finishing work! There were an infinite number of things to be done. Padma began to repeat over and over again on phone, "I cannot, I cannot . . ."

It took me a long time before I could get her to a point where we were able to talk sensibly without her acting hysterical. She did not want to disappoint Bhagwan. Disappointing Him was the greatest fear for all of us. When she finally stopped crying, I told her how she could get the absolutely necessary work completed as quickly as possible. The rest—the cosmetics and beauty work—could be done later after Bhagwan's arrival. I reassured her, asked her to not reel under pressure, and told her to see that the house was prepared for His arrival in as best a manner as possible.

I had work to do too. His flight needed to be organized. We wanted to fly Him on a charter plane from New Jersey to the airport closest to the ranch. It was not easy to charter an airplane for such a long flight duration during the weekend. I also had no cash to pay in advance. Usually such flights cost more than $15,000. I called several private airlines and finally found one that provided us with an aircraft and a pilot, just as we had wanted. I paid with my American Express Card. Fortunately, I had a high credit limit on it. Bhagwan thankfully did not understand the system of credit cards and, therefore, had not gone shopping with one.

To my surprise, everything went well. The flight was tiring but still enjoyable. It was a joyous moment for Bhagwan and me. I was proud of how far we had gotten.

I had not had any opportunity to talk to Padma and ask her for updates, so I had no idea what was waiting for us at the ranch. But I was convinced that if something was not found ready for Bhagwan, then it would be His fault, because He had put us under so much pressure. I even thought that a little discomfort would not be bad for Him. At the same time I had trust in Padma and her work. She loved Bhagwan just like I did. I knew she would have done everything in her power to complete the house. The result of this trust rewarded us when we reached the ranch. Everything turned out beautifully.

First we saw the beautifully groomed lawn in front of Bhagwan's house. Hundreds of square meters of greenery greeted when we entered it. Tall trees stood on both sides of the street which led to His house. The Sannyasins who had worked so hard to create it were all sitting quietly together, sun-tanned and in freshly washed clothes. They smiled with joy and tears in their eyes to welcome Bhagwan in His new home. Some played music.

The scene was heavenly. Bhagwan left the car and went to the Sannyasins and sat down with them in silence for a few minutes. Then He stood up smiling and went into His new house. He looked golden in His happiness. The Sannyasins were euphoric. I was drowning in my love.

I had fulfilled my second promise. I had created a new home for Him where He could build a commune of the grandest vision.

22
Security problems in this remote and inhospitable part of Oregon

After the first article about our arrival in Oregon appeared in the *Los Angeles Times*, we received our first hate letter, written with blood and with a razor blade attached to it. "Don't cross the Mason-Dixon line, otherwise you can expect something . . ." This letter was signed "KKK." After this we began to receive hate letters—many of them containing death threats—daily.

Already during our first summer the ranch had been set on fire on the Jefferson County side. We had caught red-handed four drunken cowboys, so called Rednecks (conservative, racist farmers), when they were putting the fire. When we handed them over to the state police, nothing happened. No conviction, no punishment. Setting fire to our ranch was apparently an ordinary event! Or something that no one seemed to mind.

From then on it happened several times each summer. Our property consisted of dry hills where fires could spread rapidly. We were under permanent threat by this arson. This forced us to set up a fire control centre at the highest point of the ranch and to form an ever-active team of firefighters quickly. Within a very short time we even had our own fire engines. Our fire station began to report on not only all cases of fire inside the ranch but even outside it at times. Our firefighters were a valuable support for the local troops.

Bhagwan and I were also threatened with abduction. We once received letters containing elaborate plans about abducting Bhagwan during one of His drives on the state highway. We were asked to pay a ransom of $1 million. We immediately informed the state and district police.

This time the police sprung into action. It was planned that arrests would be made on our land with our help. The whole situation reminded me of crime-thriller novels and movies. The blackmailers were arrested when they came to pick up the ransom. But, later, despite all written and recorded evidence, nothing was done. The blind, biased jury took note of the anti-Rajneesh mood of the locals and acquitted the criminals. In contrast to this, it is incredibly remarkable how easy it was for the US authorities to declare *me* guilty and to then throw *me* into the lion's den years later, even though there was never enough evidence. Unbelievable!

As if this was not enough, one day two people entered the grounds of the ranch and expressed a desire to participate in the meditations. They were housed in the tents of the participants. That night I suddenly woke up, restless and feeling that something was not right. Nothing was making any sense. I could not define my feelings clearly. And yet they were very strong. Somewhere something was not right. I called my assistants and told them what I felt. They also could not understand. They had never seen something bothering me so much. I was very restless.

We immediately checked Bhagwan's house. Everything was calm and normal. He was safe. I felt somewhat relieved, but not completely satisfied. I asked my helpers to wake up forty or fifty people and to check every corner of the ranch. Our streets soon began to hum with activity. The calm night-time atmosphere was disrupted. Numerous cars and jeeps drove around the site. Around five o'clock in the morning, we abandoned our search when nothing was found amiss. We decided to return to our beds.

But after a short time we were woken up by a call. It was from our Portland hotel. This hotel was in the main business district of Portland. It was meant for the convenience of our Sannyasins travelling to Portland from Rajneeshpuram. The hotel also accommodated other tourists. It was the head of the hotel on phone. He informed us that somebody had detonated a bomb inside its premises. Fortunately no Sannyasins had been injured in the attack, but a side wing of the hotel had been seriously damaged. The man who had detonated the bomb had been hit the hardest. The bomb had exploded right in his hands. He lost his eyesight and both the hands in the explosion.

Even this incident was not taken seriously by either the press or the police. Only the man who had injured himself badly was arrested. His accomplice was never found, neither was much effort put to locate him.

The arrested bomber confessed that he and his accomplice had first come to the ranch to ignite the bomb. But suddenly when in the middle of the night intensive activities started, they became scared and fled. They then drove to Portland to Hotel Rajneesh. The reception fortunately housed them in a room in the side wing in which no other guests were staying and which was adjacent to the fire protection wall and the fire exit door.

It appears as if the ever-sympathetic Existence protected us from this terrorist act. Even today I get anxious just thinking about that incident and what could have happened had I not woken up feeling restless. I also wonder what the real motives of the two bombers were.

If we had not taken drastic measures to protect ourselves after this incident, we would have ourselves been guilty of carelessness if an attack had happened in the future. We had understood that the police and the courts were not on our side. They were under immense public pressure. They did not want to risk their electoral votes. So, we were left in the lurch to take care of ourselves on our own. The state did not only do nothing to protect our rights, it even deliberately violated them. The barrel began to overflow when a memo from the office of the governor arrived at our doorstep. It was sent to us unofficially by one of his secretaries. This memo contained a complete plan to stage a riot in Rajneeshpuram with a motive to destroy us and our work. Involved in this plan were the governor, the attorney general, the FBI, the state police, the district police, and the National Guard. Their plan was to enter the ranch during a forthcoming festival disguised as Sannyasins, and then to ignite a riot during the satsang, when all participants of the festival were in the Rajneesh Mandir around Bhagwan.

This was a heinous, criminal plan beyond imagination. We were peaceful, joyful, loving people who took care of our affairs ourselves on our own premises. We never disturbed anybody. We did not injure anybody. We did not go from door to door selling Bibles and annoying people like the Jehovah's Witnesses. We did not give flowers to travellers at airports like the Hare Krishna monks. We had in fact cultivated a dry piece of land which was considered useless. We had injected millions of dollars into the Oregon economy. Then why such hatred?!

On Bhagwan's order I held a press conference to expose this plan. I even sent press releases to all major media houses. But nobody was willing to print or broadcast this explosive news. The Oregon press was silent; the news channels gave us the cold shoulder. Not a single investigation took place. The result of this incident was that Bhagwan ordered me to build our own force. He instructed me to look for the best militarily trained people on the ranch and train and organize them. He also asked me to acquire all automatic and sophisticated weapons possible. I told Him that legally we could only get semi-automatic ones, not the automatic kind.

According to Bhagwan, the FBI was responsible for the Jonestown tragedy. He once told me, "These self-righteous people and politicians create situations in which weak people like the Reverend Jones commit suicide. We will fight against them. We will not let them destroy us. Make that clear before the press . . . If they touch even one of us, we will catch fifteen of them. You prepare our people for this. Train them well and hard. Our people must be made better than them. And then we will show and demonstrate our strength, without hesitation. This will serve to deter people who want to make things difficult for us. Have no fear. Fire must be fought with fire. Teach a lesson to these odious people . . ."

Bhagwan's instructions were immediately put into practice. We called four trainers from three of the strongest military

243

nations of the world: Israel, Switzerland, and South Africa. We selected the best, the most trusted, and the strongest of Sannyasins for a daily training schedule of four to six hours. It was carried out under strict secrecy. The training included fitness exercises and handling of all kinds of weapons. The trainers were allowed to be tough, if necessary.

The members of this task force had no illusions. It was clear to them that they may have to sacrifice everything for the safety of Bhagwan and His people. We had carefully selected them. They were extremely devoted to Bhagwan. Their devotion had been tested by Bhagwan over the years. Some of these Sannyasins had also guarded Bhagwan's house from the new security tower built directly above His room.

Around this time, Bhagwan also instructed me to build an underground chamber for Him. This facility was to be equipped with all necessary accessories, emergency health care, and the like. The whole building was to be kept completely confidential. In a commune that literally hummed with gossip, this was no easy task. Since getting the necessary building permits would have meant letting the cat out of the bag, we decided to build something else right next to it to deflect attention.

So a swimming pool was built right behind my house. During its construction we also constructed a well-equipped and luxurious secret room for Bhagwan under my house. We even dug a tunnel under the creek connecting the highway and the room. We also planned elaborate diversionary tactics in case the government and the FBI were to succeed in inciting riots inside the commune. Right from rescuing Bhagwan from His house to getting Him out on the highway, we had every little detail planned.

The secret room was cleaned regularly, so it was always fresh, clean, and ready to use for Bhagwan. We took much pain to keep it odour free as Bhagwan was allergic to many scents.

Even though the construction of this room was kept absolutely secret, we had no sinister or criminal intentions in building and maintaining it.

The public and the politicians deemed our efforts to protect ourselves a major threat. Nobody understood that we had made all these efforts because *we* were threatened. Some cowboys from the area were already using targets with photos of Bhagwan on them for shooting practice. Posters which read "Don't hunt deer - hunt Rajneeshees!" were being sold. The local politicians were strengthening crazy prejudices in their areas against Rajneeshees. Anybody would want to protect himself and his family in such a situation. This is only natural. But, of course, when we did it, it was scandalous!

Soon, Bhagwan's afternoon drives also became a security concern. Local Jesus fanatics had joined the anti-Rajneesh group, and they would together organize demonstrations on the route which Bhagwan's car took. They would try to block the streets or even push Him from the roadway. This forced us to carry weapons visibly. We also arranged full-security escort cars that moved both in front of and behind His car. These cars were also equipped with medical emergency instruments and a radio set-up. These measures helped to hold off these threats and dangerous people.

The media around the world created a huge uproar because of the weapons that were visible on us. The public wanted to be informed about our military strength. So I finally one day called a press conference. In the presence of the regional and state police as well as the media, I presented the trained people who respectfully demonstrated the handling of their well-kept weapons. All targets were hit by them perfectly. Even James Bond would have paled from envy at the sight of their accuracy. Everyone was shocked how professionally and skillfully we had trained our soldiers.

Our secret was simple. We treated our weapons with religious devotion. Our people knew Zen. They understood the importance of martial arts, of training, and of knowing how to use their weapons correctly and deftly. They understood very well that their skills and weapons were only meant for deterrence and not for destruction.

There was never any misuse of weapons in the commune. We had to take to arms only for our defence. We just wanted the freedom to live our existence. This was our existential right. But despite our repeated clarifications and reassurances, the government remained hostile. Laws were always used against us, or at least to limit and inhibit us. And if some of the existing laws were in our favour, they were changed by the government quickly.

It was a constant struggle to always be a bit ahead of the authorities. The cat and mouse game had to be played by us day in and day out. I began to remain worried. Bhagwan sensed my anxiety. He called me and said, "Remind the people that we are not violent. We are forced to bear arms . . . We must do this with utmost awareness. No one should touch the weapons when angry . . . Be meditative before you start the training. Before you touch weapons, make the Gachchhamis (our daily prayers). Then begin the training. Then when you are done, you must again do Gachchhamis in order to give thanks for the training."

He told a beautiful story once . . .

Once there was a great Zendo master. He was eighty, and traditionally, the disciple who could defeat him would succeed him. So all the disciples hoped that someday he would accept their challenge, because now he was getting old.

There was one disciple who was the cleverest, the best strategist, very powerful, but not a master of Zendo, just skilled in the art. Although he was a good warrior and he knew everything about swordsmanship, he was not yet a pillar of energy, he was still afraid while fighting. The tathata had not yet happened to him.

He went to the master again and again saying, "Now the time has come, and you are getting old. Soon you will be too old to challenge at all. I challenge you now. Accept my challenge, Master, and give me a chance to show what I have learned from you." The master laughed and avoided him.

The disciple started thinking that the master had become so weak and old that he was afraid, just trying to evade the challenge. So one night he insisted and insisted and got angry and said, "I will not leave until you accept my challenge. Tomorrow morning you have to accept. You are getting old and soon there will be no chance for me to show what I have learned from you. This has been a tradition always."

The master said, "If you insist, your very insistence shows that you are not ready or prepared. There is too much excitement in you, your ego wants to challenge, you have not yet become capable; but if you insist, okay. Do one thing. Go to the nearby monastery where there is a monk who was my disciple ten years ago. He became so efficient in Zendo that he threw away his sword and became a sannyasin. He was my rightful successor. He never challenged me, and he was the only one who could have challenged and even defeated me. So first go and challenge that monk. If you can defeat him, then come to me. If you cannot defeat him, then just drop the idea."

The disciple immediately started out for the monastery. By morning he was there. He challenged the monk. He couldn't believe that this monk could be a Zendo master — lean and thin, continuously meditating, eating only once a day. The monk listened and laughed, and he said, "You have come to give me a challenge? Even your master cannot challenge me, even he is afraid."

Listening to this, the disciple got completely mad! He said, "Stand up immediately! Here is a sword I have brought for you knowing well that you are a monk and might not have one. Come out in the garden. This is insulting, and I will not listen."

The monk looked absolutely undisturbed. He said, "You are just a child, you are not a warrior. You will be killed immediately. Why are you asking for death unnecessarily?"

That made him still angrier so they both went out. The monk said, "I will not need the sword, because a real master never needs it. I am not going to attack you; I am only going to give you a chance to attack me till your sword is broken. You are not a match for me. You are a child, and people will laugh at me if I take up the sword against you."

It was too much! The young man jumped up — but then he saw that the monk was standing. Up until now the monk had been sitting; now he stood up, closed his eyes, and started swaying from side to side — and suddenly the young man saw that the monk had disappeared. There was only a pillar of energy — no face, just a solid pillar of energy, swaying. He became afraid and started retreating, and the pillar of energy started moving towards him, swaying. He threw away his sword and screamed at the top of his voice, "Save me!"

The monk sat down again and started laughing. His face came back, the energy disappeared, and he said, "I told you before: even your master is no match for me. Go and tell him."

Perspiring, trembling, nervous, the disciple went back to his master and said, "How grateful I am for your compassion towards me. I am no match for you. Even that monk destroyed me completely. But one thing I couldn't tolerate, that is why I got so involved in it. He said, 'Even your master is not a match for me.'"

The master started laughing and said, "So that rascal played the trick on you too? You got angry? Then he could see through you, because anger is a hole in the being. And that has become his basic trick. Whenever I send somebody to him, he starts talking against me, and my disciples of course become angry. When they are angry, he finds out that they have loopholes, and when you have holes you cannot fight."

(From "Wholeness," in *Osho: The Empty Boat*)

23
Bhagwan: a saint or just an ordinary man?

Bhagwan was gorgeous. Exceedingly beautiful. The king of my heart. But He was not too unlike other men. In fact, He had many weaknesses of the ordinary man. This understanding of Him helped me a lot in dealing with Him objectively. We chatted like good friends. He could talk with me openly about His problems and wishes without having to worry about anything.

Bhagwan suffered from the same domestic problems as every married man. Toothache made Him grumpy. Bad weather made Him depressed. He nagged when things did not run as He wanted them to run. There were days when He behaved as if nobody could do anything right for Him. On such days He needed me. He loved me. He trusted me. I was able to reassure Him by just being present. He felt safe with me just as I felt safe in His presence.

The winter of 1981 was our first winter on the ranch in Oregon. When buying the land in the summer we had no idea about the difficulties that winters were going to bring.

A beautiful creek ran directly through our land. Bhagwan's place was set up on the more isolated side of this creek, in one of the most beautiful valleys of the ranch. My house was situated a little further above, on the other side of the creek. So that we could reach from one shore to the other easily, we built a dam over it.

One day a once-in-a-century rain occurred simultaneously with snowmelt, and the dam broke. The water crashed down at a monstrous speed. Bhagwan's house was beautifully located, but this beauty had its price. Now, because of the broken dam, He was cut off from us and from civilization. Bad weather does not spare anyone, not even an enlightened one.

Incidentally, that day, Bhagwan was in a bad mood. Vivek, who took care of His personal needs and behaved as if she were married to Him, had been arguing with Him about His love affair with other women. She was extremely jealous of all the other women who approached Him. In her mad jealousy, she often tried to even blackmail Him. She would yell and threaten to leave Him and then destroy Him by telling the world about the truth of their relationship. I found the kind of truth that she had in mind not so damaging. Many women go through such a phase in their lives.

Vivek lived with Him as His wife. They had sexual contact. He insisted that she always use contraceptives. He had made it clear that He did not want any children. He did not believe in either marriage or in raising children.

One day, back in 1978, when we were still in Poona, she wanted to teach Him a lesson because for a long time He had not shown any interest in her. She had sex with Him without using contraceptives and became pregnant. This was a very scandalous situation in India, especially for a holy man like Bhagwan. His followers had often claimed that He was a celibate. That is expected of saints, particularly in India.

Fortunately, one of His dedicated Sannyasins was a prominent gynaecologist in Poona. He also owned a private clinic for women. With his help, Vivek's pregnancy problem was solved quickly. She had an abortion, and then sterilization. This was no big deal. This doctor regularly performed abortions for Sannyasins and the women of Poona. Birth control was promoted and abortions were legal under the government of Indira Gandhi to address the problem of overpopulation.

Laxmi very quickly organized an abortion and sterilization date for Vivek. I was in her room when she called the doctor. The event was being completely hushed up. Only Bhagwan, Dr Saraswati (the gynaecologist), Laxmi, and I knew what was really going on. Everyone in the Lao-Tsu House was walking as on egg shells. They had just been told that Vivek was not well. Laxmi asked me to look serious when visiting Vivek in her room. Laxmi was quite worried because of this matter and felt it could be risky to trust just anyone. But she trusted me in such situations.

So, Vivek had used her womb as a weapon against Bhagwan. He decided that He had had enough of her. Shortly thereafter, He threw her out from His bedroom and had no sexual contact with her anymore. Bhagwan asked her to get a boyfriend with whom she could play such manipulative games which she was so fond of.

Vivek still constantly kept nagging. He would often complain to me about her behaviour. Once He even tried to send her back to England after promising to provide her with everything she would need to live comfortably there. But He was not lucky. After four days she came back from England, weeping.

Vivek had never liked the ranch in Oregon. She in fact did not like most things in life. In Oregon, she did not get as much attention from Him as before and was bored. To be content was not in her make up. Being happy would not have allowed her the control over Bhagwan that she desired so much. So she preferred to be suicidal.

On this stormy and rainy day, Bhagwan had not only had a dispute with Vivek, He also had toothache. He was miserable. Moreover, He was desperate to drive. Because of bad roads and worse weather, He had not been able to drive His cars for a whole week.

I heard of the broken dam early in the morning when I was still asleep. I was instantly wide awake and began to take stock of the situation. Soon a message came via radio that I should immediately report to Bhagwan. I told Vivek that this was impossible. The water was very high and there was a strong current too. It was a very dangerous creek to cross at that time. Even if I were to order a helicopter from Portland, it would not have been able to reach the ranch. And even if it would have, it would have taken several hours to complete the journey. Bhagwan had no sympathy for these circumstances. He wanted to see me urgently. I joked: "Even if I ride a horse, it would take me two hours . . ."

So He demanded that I come to Him on a horse! And He was a man who had never been able to take no for an answer.

We had four wild horses. They belonged to the ranch. They were pretty wild and not meant for riding. They had not been properly trained. But I mounted myself on one of them. We took the pass over the mountains to get to Bhagwan's house. It was appalling. The horse did not want to move in this bad weather, let alone carry a weight around. Fortunately, I was not very heavy.

At times the path was very narrow. Once it was even less than one meter wide. It was extremely scary. While on one side there was a wall of rock, on the other side there was a raging creek about twenty to thirty meters below. If the horse had taken even one wrong step, we would both have fallen down the abyss never to return. We managed to cross the creek at a shoal. It was difficult to force a creature acting on instinct to step into dangerously flowing water. But I somehow managed it.

I landed at Bhagwan's house in the middle of a domestic dispute between Vivek and Him. He told me He really had had enough of her. He said that Vivek irritated and tormented Him and that He had a toothache and wanted to drive His Rolls-Royce. He requested me to manage to get rid of the woman. "Buy her a ticket to England and ensure that she leaves immediately. I cannot tolerate her presence for one more second." I said I would do my best. When I returned to my house in the afternoon, I found a message from Him. Vivek had apologized and He wanted to give her another chance.

From this incident I learned several lessons. Firstly, that Bhagwan was a man with ordinary feelings. Secondly, that I must make sure that He was never cut off from the outside world due to any disaster. Third, even an enlightened one cannot get rid of a woman! The reality is that neither can a man can live with a woman, nor can he live without her.

I allowed Him thereafter to simply be a man. I did not put Him on any pedestal. He was certainly a god, the god of my heart, but not the Creator. I did not want to suffocate Him by wanting to make Him perfect. I let Him breathe. I let Him fart. I had sympathy for His sexual urges of springtime. It was all easy for me: in my eyes He was simply a handsome, intelligent, and desirable man.

I let Him have His fun.

24

What is the antidote for Bhagwan's boredom? Thirty new Rolls-Royces!

As we settled into the routine of the commune in Oregon, more and more Sannyasins began to come to live, work, and meditate with us. Soon our newly built city was thriving with thousands of Sannyasins. In Rajneeshpuram there were around five thousand commune members living. When we had our big festival, we'd have around fifteen thousand visiting Sannyasins from around the world, living with us for about one to six weeks.

Among these there were those who were serious about our mission, and there were escapists too; there were hard workers taking refuge from the stress and strain of their previous lives, and there were egotists looking for recognition and glory too. There were some who felt they were more privileged than others and demanded to be treated as such, and then there were some who used meditation as an excuse to not participate in the hard work of developing the commune further. And then there were those who were purposeless, merely hangers-on.

To put an order to this chaotic mess, Bhagwan decided to make some changes in the structure of the commune. He asked all privileges to be taken away from the Sannyasins who had been enjoying them. The privileges were always related to Bhagwan: front seat at His discourses, darshan at His house, and things like that. This announcement was music to my ears. I had never liked the separation between privileged and ordinary Sannyasins. When we were in Poona, these so-called special people would fight, order around, and upset His innocent followers. They would pollute the atmosphere of joy and love around Bhagwan with their pretentious meditative attitude. Fortunately this all was going to stop now, and we were going to have a healthier commune.

Bhagwan became very strict at this time. Pretentious spirituality was no longer tolerated by Him. Hard work became the new motto. The new orders were: work and only then have fun. The development of the commune became the first priority. His staff was reduced to a minimum. Old hangers-on, who were a pain in the neck, were removed, and He surrounded Himself with new people. He wanted to see happy faces around. He had had enough of being surrounded by serious, frowning faces pretending to be meditative.

He wanted every Sannyasin to work equally hard. He no longer wanted around useless people, whose laziness could be contagious. Meditation was appreciated by Him, but Sannyasins who convulsed while meditating annoyed Him. He also did not want to have any guards close by any more. He preferred to have a bit of fresh air around His nose. He told me, "Seela, you stop this nonsense with the bodyguards and samurais. They have become lazy and outrageous. They get on my nerves. They exploit other Sannyasins . . ."

Question: Why are the ashramite sannyasins not allowed to participate in all meditations? Why are they told to participate in only one meditation every day?

Answer: But they would like to do all the meditations just to avoid the work. A few are absolutely lazy and they think that they can rationalize it. For example, let me tell you about one day in one Sannyasin's life. From six to seven in the morning he will meditate, then comes breakfast. Then eight to nine-thirty or ten is the lecture. Then of course by ten o'clock he has already done too much: meditated, listened to such a long lecture…. So a little gossiping — it is obviously needed. Then by eleven, eleven-thirty, he is ready for lunch. By twelve, of course, he has already done too much — meditating, listening, and even eating — so by twelve o'clock he goes to sleep. Up till three o'clock, rest is needed. Three to three-thirty: tea or coffee time. Three-thirty to four-thirty: Nadabrahma, an individual meditation. Four-thirty to five-thirty he goes for a walk of course. One needs a little physical exercise. Five-thirty to six-thirty: Kundalini meditation. Then dinner time. And then, of course, the girlfriend comes, so the day is complete. Still more meditations you need? …They are told not to meditate too much because listening to me is meditation. Can you do a better meditation than listening to me? If you love the work, if you love me, that is meditation. Your whole life should be meditation. People who come for a few days from the outside have to learn meditation, but those who are living in the ashram — their whole life should be meditation. Their walking, their sitting, even their sleep; everything should become meditative. Meditation should be a climate here. Not something that you do, but something that you are….

(From "Are You the Greatest Master?," in *Osho: Come Follow To You, Vol 2*)

He also expressed His displeasure at the various sects that had formed in the commune. He told me to let everybody know that in His commune nobody had any special position anymore. Only He was to be special. He gave a clear message that *He* was the master, not the Teerthas and Somendras of the commune. Teertha and Somendra were privileged Sannyasins and prominent therapists; both were skilled at using their therapy participants to satiate their desire for the material.

Such messages led to a lot of gossip, but this did not bother Him. It was His commune. No other master was needed. Only His leadership was required. He needed no one to give Him advice. He was the only one to give instructions, He made this absolutely clear.

He hated questions like "Is Teertha enlightened?" or "Is Somendra a master?" and detested letters describing a strong energy that Sannyasins had felt near Vivek during discourses. If anybody showed more loyalty or interest in somebody other than Him, He ordered me to either get that person's head straight or take their Mala away and throw them out.

He also did not like when the principles of the commune were questioned or when its functioning was criticized. Even if it was never publicly acknowledged, Bhagwan was the force behind all the rules. For legal reasons we had created an impression that He did not have the slightest clue about our worldly affairs. In reality, however, the smallest of instructions came from Him.

One day He called some of us to a meeting, an important meeting. Along with some people from His house, my two trusted assistants, Vidya and Savita, were also present at this meeting. Vidya was a blonde from South Africa, a bundle of energy. She was very talented and effortlessly defied all those nasty jokes about blondes. Vidya, Savita, and I functioned as one unit. We together were the management team. I took care of Bhagwan and His madness, Savita cared for the enormous finances, and Vidya organized workers, good as well as the bad ones.

On this day Bhagwan looked very solemn. He was in no mood for any nonsense. He began with the words, "I have called you all here to explain a few things to you. Listen carefully. Seela, you have to protect my commune and my people. Savita, you and Vidya help Seela with this. It is the most difficult task that I am giving to you. It will not be easy. It will bring much hostility. Many people will try to prevent you from your work. But, you have to defend my teaching, you must protect it. You must protect my teaching and my commune even from myself . . ."

I felt deeply worried by this announcement. I was already working very hard. Now I was required to do even more. Not only *do*, but even *remember* every moment how valuable His teachings were. Now I had to prove that I was worthy of my job. This was no small responsibility. To protect His teachings meant first of all to understand them, incorporate them into everything, and then to act accordingly. I had understood what He wanted from me. Even today after so many years, I live according to His expectations from me. I live according to His teachings. I have incorporated His entire oeuvre in my daily life. This is not a conscious effort. It just is. His teachings have become a part of me.

Shortly after this conversation a nightmarish situation arose where I had to choose between His demands and what was good for the commune.

In the commune, at this time, everything was working very

well. Even the centres in Europe were running beautifully. The last chapter of His dream had started. The Rajneesh Academy and a library building were already in the pipeline. Books were being published on schedule, festivals were being planned and then executed well. The controversies in the press and television were at an all-time high, and we were in the spotlight big time. New sources for donations were being discovered every day. Everything was going exactly according to His ideas.

But Bhagwan was not excited or happy. Perhaps everything was going on too well. He was getting bored. So one day, out of the blue, He demanded of me to get Him thirty new Rolls-Royces within one month. At this time He already had ninety-six brand new Rolls-Royces. Obviously He was only looking for entertainment.

Thirty Rolls-Royces meant about three to four million dollars. We could have arranged this kind of money only by drastically reducing our operating budget. This meant that I could have fulfilled His wish only by cutting down the expenses for the basic needs of the residents of not only Rajneeshpuram but also all other communes. These other communes formed an essential part of His work and supported His teachings. For the Sannyasins living in them there were no luxuries anyway. Luxuries were reserved only for Bhagwan and His household.

I felt torn. I loved Bhagwan immensely, but the commune was my child, and I had to protect it according to His instructions. How could I decide against either one of them?

This conflict threw me back to His teachings. "If you have difficulties making a decision, choose the lesser of the two evils." For me, in this case, that was refusing to get His new Rolls-Royces.

When I told Him this, He became bad tempered. My refusal became yet one more reason for Him to procure these cars. He decided to change His tactics.

Next day I received a list from Him with fifty to sixty names. He asked me to invite these people to a meeting to take place the very next day in His living room. I immediately knew what He was up to when I saw the names of the people on that list. Most of them were quite rich. My heart sank. By now, I had become familiar with these indirect attacks by Him. I had no choice but to obey.

The invited Sannyasins were very excited. They began to imagine that they were special. On receiving the news, they acted as if they were better than everyone else. They expressed no qualms when they were stuffed into a room that had space only for thirty people for the meeting. When one feels important, then even a bit of inconvenience seems more tolerable to them.

In the meeting, as always, I sat at Bhagwan's feet. I decided to fall asleep to show my displeasure. My conduct was one of obvious rebellion. Later I was scolded by Him for this act. I found it necessary to act like this as I had had enough of being manipulated by Him.

Bhagwan had manipulated me and others many times before that day, but never had He done it in such an explicit and obvious manner. There was no spirituality anymore, only exploitation and more exploitation of all His followers. I had always tried to learn from His actions, but that day it felt clearly like abuse. The whole tone was dishonest. I had never expected this kind of undignified behaviour from Him.

He began, "The time has come. I will soon leave my body . . ."

I said to myself, "Not again. Not this!" I knew exactly what was to follow. I had listened to such speeches many times before that day. He had used this tactic in the discourses too. There it was not bad. But here, in that way! I heard someone sob. Inwardly, I was cringing. I strongly wanted to stand up and leave, but I did not do it because I did not want to insult Him in public.

As expected, twenty-one people were declared enlightened. They were now a part of "the inner circle" that was to lead His commune and the Sannyasins after His death. I should not be the one to manage it alone, He was clear on this front. He never asked me though whether after His death I would still want to be in the commune, be a part of the whole madness. But the agenda here was different: emptying pockets and accounts for thirty new Rolls-Royces. A large sum was at stake, and so the enticement had to be greater as well.

An hour later I was really fed up. The meeting had ended, but I still could not leave. I had to survive another meeting with the freshly enlightened whose well-loaded wallets needed to be emptied. He had staged this show for *them*. This meeting was even more uncomfortable for me. He told them that He saw an opportunity to postpone His leaving His body. They only had to get Him some cars. This new attachment would keep His body on the earth.

In this meeting He attacked me directly: "Poor Seela is not responsible. She has to take care of the commune and its needs. I cannot put more on her. For her, it would be easier to lead the commune without me. There would be fewer disputes when I would be no longer in my body . . ." He carried on for forty to fifty minutes in this tone until He saw that His audience was prepared to get Him everything He wanted to prolong His stay on earth. I wanted to go out and throw up.

This meeting led to the results He desired.

I was angry. I could not close my eyes even for one moment that night. I had had enough of all the cars and the fancy watches of the world.

The next morning, I had to drive Him to the Buddha Hall for a discourse. For the first time, I did not look forward to being with Him. During the trip, we did not speak a word to each other. We did not even wish each other good morning. He did not ask me how I was doing, and I just drove the car. On our way to the hall and back, we both observed that some Sannyasins were behaving very strangely. They were touching the feet of those who had been declared enlightened the previous day. I laughed loudly. He asked me what was going on. That was my chance to rub salt into His open wounds.

I told Him of the parties that had taken place the previous night in the houses of the newly enlightened Sannyasins. They had celebrated their enlightenment extravagantly. The whole commune was humming with gossip. The newly enlightened were already gathering their disciples and holding court. Only three among the "enlightened" had not participated in this circus.

One of these three was a very special man. He was an old Sannyasin, both old in age and in experience as a Sannyasin. He was a personal friend of Bhagwan. Being an Indian politician and a former member of the Indian Parliament, he had an important status in the commune. He was devoted to Bhagwan and had not hesitated in being initiated by Him. He had left his home and had given up his job to move into the ashram in Poona and to be with Bhagwan. Bhagwan had given him a new name: Swami Maitreya. He was joyful and thankful to everybody.

That morning I also told Bhagwan what Swami Maitreya had said about the previous day's meeting: "What is this nonsense, that He declares all these people enlightened?" I thought He didn't hear me because He did not reply. He simply became very angry and ordered me to immediately call together these people and beat some sense into their heads.

A few months after this event, Bhagwan spoke about the ego of the "enlightened" ones and also about their enlightenment. He hit them very hard. He never missed an opportunity for such hits. He hated it when people behaved like Him. He did not like Sannyasins worshipping other Sannyasins. To see them touching each other's feet infuriated Him. In this discourse, He spoke very positively about Maitreya and his simple heart. He quoted Maitreya and declared such enlightenment nonsense.

After this discourse Maitreya came to me surprised. He said, "So nothing that you know can be hidden from Bhagwan! You're certainly a good chronicler of what goes on . . ." I answered that I was also surprised that Bhagwan had not only heard what I had reported to Him but had also developed a very good opinion of him as a result.

It was often like that. He solved a problem and then caused another one, which I then had to fix. He flattered their egos, and I had to dismantle them afterwards. It was teamwork.

I had become an expert in executing His instructions precisely to the letter. That made me a prime target for negativity and anger. Meanwhile He could maintain His gentle and loving role. I was the perfect garbage dump where everyone was able to unload their negativity. I had to play the bad bitch.

25
Meet the Fourth Estate's puppet and puppeteer

From time to time Bhagwan held personal meetings with certain important Sannyasins to give them direct instructions. He would repeatedly tell them not to argue with me, because I acted precisely according to His directives.

Throughout the development of Rajneeshpuram, Bhagwan was always kept well informed about whatever was happening in the commune down to the smallest detail. Everything was planned and executed under His direct supervision. But we protected Him from all legal entanglements through His silence. He led the entire commune from behind His silence. Therefore such personal meetings with Sannyasins were risky from a legal point of view because they hinted at Bhagwan's direct involvement in the administration of the commune.

Rajneeshpuram was a kind of state with Bhagwan as its religious head. It was best for Him not to be involved with the government of the state. State and religion should not intermingle.

Before Sannyasins were taken to Bhagwan for a private rendezvous, we explained to them that they were getting a very rare privilege. They were warned in advance that if they discussed any aspect of the meeting or reported to someone else about its content, they would never have a second opportunity. But despite such detailed instructions, many Sannyasins would tell their friends about it. And even if nothing was said about the meeting, others would often be able to put two and two together, when a Sannyasin would shower at half past six in the morning, dress meticulously, come to my house, and drive away with me in my car. It did not take a leap of imagination to guess where the person was going. Moreover when these Sannyasins returned from the visit, they would be radiating with joy, making the cause of their absence very obvious. So it was always difficult to hide as big an event as a meeting with Bhagwan from other residents. To be able to see Him was an unparalleled gift and a privilege. I understood how valuable it was to the Sannyasins who got this opportunity. Therefore I never had the heart to take this gift away from anyone even though the whole affair was perennially riddled with risk and danger and despite the fact that some Sannyasins behaved over-enthusiastically.

There was one advantage of these meetings for me: Bhagwan made it clear to the Sannyasins whom He met that I was on no ego or power trip. In these meetings, they learned that I was simply a puppet dancing to His tunes.

Bhagwan was also the chief architect of our media strategy. He meticulously choreographed all my appearances in media. What would I say, how I should say it, when I should say it—everything was scripted by Him.

Bhagwan and I always watched together the video recordings of every television news program about us. This kept us up to date about the opinions expressed in the media pertaining to us. Bhagwan also thoroughly reviewed each of my television appearances. The dates as well as the content of our conferences were planned meticulously by Him.

These appearances were important to Bhagwan because, according to Him, they were the best and the cheapest means of advertising for us. Their purpose was to create as much controversy as possible by making extravagant claims and inflammatory statements in an extremely obnoxious and provocative manner. This was aimed at raising curiosity about us in the public and to attract more and more Sannyasins and donors towards us.

So our media strategy was completely controversy-driven. The media and the masses are not interested in either truth or good. They only want scandals and sensations. TV ratings and audience demand are the only things that count. What is most important is to ensure that the public does not stay indifferent. Restraint and niceties have no place in TV, newspapers, and magazines. Fire and fireworks are essential for their profits.

A notable instance of the implementation of this strategy was my appearances on Australian TV and especially my infamous interview with Ted Koppel where I used many colourful expressions and even the four-letter word. I did not mean to be disrespectful to Ted. As a matter of fact I had a very high regard for him. But I had a job to do, and I think I did it very well.

My friends, relatives, Sannyasins, and well-wishers had problems with my conduct in these TV shows and interviews. They all felt that I was unduly nasty and obnoxious in them and that I was not portraying a very flattering image of myself.

I was never like that in person. But they could not understand that it was not my personal choice; I had nothing to say in the matter. I had a boss, a director. I was simply playing a role He had scripted for me. He was the scriptwriter. And I was an actress with a very difficult role to play. All along I acted like a hollow bamboo, willing to let Him play His music through me.

While others found my conduct outrageous, Bhagwan found me too mild and soft. I was neither enough fiery, nor enough controversial for Him. The following dialogues illustrate very well how He felt I should have played my role.

Question: Beloved Bhagwan, … during the time you didn't speak, Sheela was speaking all over the place, and many people got offended with her comments. And everybody asks, "How come Sheela is your spokesperson? How come Sheela makes those statements? She is antagonizing people." Would you say something about that?

Answer: I was also very much offended by Sheela.

Whenever she came back, I hit her hard, because she was not the way I would like her to be – really outrageous! She was falling below the standard. And I was continuously telling her, "Don't be worried, we don't have anything to lose. We have the whole world to gain and nothing to lose. Be outrageous!" There is a saying that "No news is good news." It is only half, the other half I have to make. If no news is good news, then good news is no news! It has to be sensational. I have been sharpening her like a sword. "Go, and cut as many heads as you like."

Isabel, I agree. I was also offended.

(From "The Fruits Are Ripe," in *Osho: The Last Testament, Vol 1*)

Question: Your personal secretary, Sheela, created an incredible impact in Western Australia. She was probably the number one entertainment for about a month on radio and television over there. But I understand that you are a little bit unhappy with the way she handled things. You thought she could have been a bit tougher.

Answer: She could have been.

Question: I don't believe it.

Answer: And I have been very tough with her because I don't see any limits anywhere. You can go in any direction infinitely. Sheela is not ever going to satisfy me. She is doing her best, but I would like her to do a little more . . . more.

(From "Be Ready," in *Osho: The Last Testament, Vol 1*)

Bhagwan was a lion who could roar very loud. He was not afraid of either scandals or public opinion. Fact and fiction made no difference to Him. He would think of an appropriate story and simply execute it. That's why He also introduced such an ugly, dirty scandal into the world after I left Him.

At first I was not able to understand His strategy. I did not like many of the statements I had to present to the press at press conferences. The role that I had to play did not suit my nature. My true nature is not aggressive. I do not like unnecessary conflicts or tensions. I'm a lover, not a fighter. I am caring, not offensive. So I had to first learn to understand Bhagwan's approach and as always make peace with it.

Today many journalists find me soft and gentle. I then explain to them that I am no longer Bhagwan's secretary or puppet. I no longer play a role. I don't have to protect any commune against a hostile Oregon anymore. That I really am like this. To create controversies is an art that I learned from my master. I used it very effectively at the time. Now, I have no use for it.

26
Why democracy does not work

Bhagwan was an intelligent man, confident in His judgments and decisions. He had His life well organized and chose His secretaries Himself. He neither needed advice from anyone else nor a confirmation of His choice. If someone criticized His secretary, He became angry. He took it personally. He tolerated no comments or criticism about His choices.

When I would bring letters to Him in which doubts about me were expressed, He would refuse to listen. He would become so angry that He would not want me to answer them at all. He would simply tell me to throw such letters into the bin. If within a short time He received several such letters, He would speak on this subject in His discourse and personally set the heads of the whiney Sannyasins straight. Doubts and accusations were common in our commune. Whenever someone's ego was hurt or when one felt that things were not running as they wanted, then it was time for them to blame Sheela.

I once asked Him, "Why can Sannyasins not believe that I forward your answers verbatim? Is something wrong with me? Am I doing something wrong?"

He replied, "That is easy. They are jealous of you. To be my secretary is not easy. Everybody accuses you, including me. If you get to bear my cross, you also get to be crucified for me . . ."

Many different people from all sorts of ways of life came to Bhagwan, and most of them brought their own ideas with them. However, those who came purely out of love had it easiest to understand and follow Him. Their mind did not work hard, and so they could devote themselves to Him. Those who brought their intellect, their value judgments, and firm opinions with them had it the hardest. And they also became problems themselves. The people who came to exploit others were themselves exploited. They would become disillusioned and leave. People who came only because it was fashionable to do so disappeared with the currents of fashion. Spirituality-seekers and those eager for enlightenment remained until their egos were crushed.

Unfortunately, I had to deal with such people all the time. They were miserably bad workers. They wrote so many letters questioning, arguing, and complaining to Bhagwan that if compiled they would fill volumes of books. They narrated irritating descriptions about how their energy steadily climbs during meditation and about the kind of lights they see. They wanted to have all this confirmed by Bhagwan. If they were rich Bhagwan sometimes confirmed it. This happened during public discourses. Sometimes He declared such people enlightened on the spot. Or He talked in public that their third or fourth eye had opened and that various blue and pink sparks are emitted by them sometimes. Once the purpose was achieved—meaning their pockets were emptied—He would become angry at them. And when He had had enough of a person, He would speak about it openly in the same discourses.

Bhagwan also did not believe in democracy. Whenever I would bring Him complaints of Sannyasins about the hierarchy existing in the commune, He would become very angry. Once, He said to me, "Seela, this is something you have to understand precisely. Democracy does not work. It only gives power to those who stand at the lowest. This degrades quality of life. A democracy is determined by the masses. The masses are mediocre. Their decision is not intelligent. Only ten percent of the people on the earth are intelligent. The administrative powers must be given to the person who is qualified to do it. Decisions have to be made by people who are suited for the role and understand complexities. Don't listen to those people who only want to make complaints. They don't understand my work. They don't understand me. They are not intelligent. The mentality of the masses has no place in our commune. Here decisions are made by you according to my vision of the future. I will see to it that you decide correctly. It is *my* and not their task to see whether you do your job properly or not. I will not tolerate any mediocrity in my commune . . ."

Hard work was always a basic problem for the so-called spiritual ones or meditators. But I had to tolerate them just as Laxmi, Bhagwan's former secretary, did. Work did not make one extraordinary. As a worker you could not collect disciples around yourself. Nobody waited for you. Nobody touched your feet. Nobody gave you expensive gifts. It was more rewarding to be a meditator or a therapist, than to be a worker.

For many people in the commune work was not connected to spirituality. Spirituality meant shaking rising energy, seeing light, and having many different eyes that could open. You could not show off by being merely a worker. Nobody put you on a high throne. In my opinion, these so-called spiritual ones had failed to grow out of their children's chairs. How unfortunate for them that they simply did not know how good it felt when one has really worked hard and is sweating from hard work. They did not know the good ol' joy of working.

Labour was for the unspiritual ones like me. When Rajneeshpuram was under construction and we were only working and not meditating, some Sannyasins wrote letters to Bhagwan complaining about the kind of work they were forced to do or their number of working hours. He was not very happy with such an attitude. He would roll His eyes in mock horror and tell me to be tough with these Sannyasins and ask them to either work or leave the commune.

To constantly have to set straight the heads of such Sannyasins did not make me popular in the commune. I was accused of being on a power trip. But such opinions did not divert me from my work. My loyalty belonged to Bhagwan, not to the image I was forced to project. I knew myself; I was well aware who I was and why I was there. My responsibilities were more important to me than hymns of praise.

In a way, the mass mentality, the hollow spirituality, and a failure to understand the true spirit of the Rajneesh Movement and the importance of hard work ultimately led to the downfall of the commune.

27
The final curtain falls

During and after my time in Rajneeshpuram, there was much talk about my so-called "power trip", despite the fact that I had left the commune and my powers so easily. Nobody really saw that! After I left, amazingly Bhagwan, especially, spoke in great detail on this subject. He seemed to derive pleasure out of doing this. This was perhaps an inevitable fate for all His secretaries.

I have never looked back and don't want to look back now. I had power, but it was based on love. I was given the position of high priestess in the commune only because of my profound devotion to Bhagwan. Yes, of course, I could have used this power for a lot of things, but I did not do that. I only worked and worked really hard. I was the commune mother, and I loved my children.

Bhagwan sent some messages—both public and private—to me asking me to return to Him. He wanted to forgive me and offer my position back to me. I did not return because I had done nothing for which to accept forgiveness. I had never desired the position that He was offering me again. Power was

276

never interesting or important for me. I had just followed what Existence had wished for me. I know that I served Bhagwan as well as I could in all honesty, openness, selflessness, and love.

In His own words:

Sheela has done much good, ninety-nine percent good. The whole credit of keeping the entire commune together, of creating houses for five thousand people with all the modern facilities, with central air conditioning – I don't think any city is totally air-conditioned as you are – of giving you the best food possible . . . She has done immense good to you, and you should be grateful for it.

(From "Existential Worship," in *Osho: From Bondage to Freedom*)

For me, the time had come to go away from Him and start my own life. This is why I left. There was nothing mysterious in it. It was simply my destiny. The right thing at the right time. Just like Bhagwan, I did not want to go back in life.

I was often asked by many, "You were left standing out in the cold all by yourself by Bhagwan and His people with a bag full of debt. Were you not angry or bitter?"

My reply to such questions has always been, "I could have felt like this, but I loved Him. I was, am His disciple. I have learned to accept. I understand His anger, His sadness."

To point finger at others is the easiest way to ease pain and sorrow. But I accepted everything that happened to me without anger or resentment. For many, blaming others is the best way to forget losses. The whole world works like that. The whole world is full of blame and accusations. But Bhagwan's teachings do not support these vices.

I have never felt that leaving Bhagwan and the commune was a mistake, otherwise I would have had no problem in returning and apologizing to everyone when Bhagwan called me later. I have never had a problem admitting my mistakes. In fact I openly admit my mistakes because I see them as milestones on my way to growth and success. Bhagwan had prepared us in such a way that we could stand on our own two feet when the time came. I did exactly this. When I felt the time had come, I parted ways and ventured out on my own.

This one incident, which happened sometime in 1983 in my private life, also had a huge public impact. In a fit of anger and frustration I hit a man whom I loved. It was an impulsive reaction with its roots in a far deeper anger. Immediately after this moment of freaking out, I realized what I had done. I said, "Oh my God, what have I done? How could I do such a thing?" Thankfully I had the courage at that time to immediately apologize and ask for his forgiveness.

The impact of this incident was not small for me or for what I represented. In normal life this act would have had no great importance. But for me, the head of the commune and high priestess of the religion, it was simply not acceptable. I had exercised violence against another person, against a Sannyasin, a member of our commune. I had dishonoured Bhagwan. I had disobeyed His teaching: *be aware, be conscious, be watchful*. Violence of any kind was forbidden in Rajneeshpuram.

I, in a moment of craziness and anger, had committed this grave mistake, and it was not easy for me to live with it. I suffered. I was deeply ashamed and had hardly the courage to face Him again. For this crime, I was ready to accept any punishment that Bhagwan or Existence would have imposed on me. I no longer felt worthy of being His secretary. I could not concentrate on work until I had told Him everything.

I saw Bhagwan the same evening. He immediately saw my red, swollen eyes. Luckily He did not let me suffer very long. He showed compassion and asked, "What is going on, Seela?"

I burst into tears. I described to Him in minute detail what I had done and how I felt about it. He bent down, put His compassionate hand on my head, and said, "I forgive you. You have understood. I forgive you, but now you must ask the commune for forgiveness . . ."

I did it. I bowed down to the whole commune and asked for forgiveness. The Sannyasins were generous. They immediately forgave me. They shared my pain, my tears. The next day I received mountains of love letters. Many people were touched by my open apology and my courage. I felt then that it was time to forgive myself. And even though I did forgive myself soon, I have never been able to forget this slip. Since that day, I am always very careful with my anger. Even today, this incident is always present in my heart and guides me in moments of frustration and anger.

After I left the commune, it was clear that those who assumed management of His life failed to follow both His teachings and wishes. He was arrested. Revenge and harassment were the two primary motives for sending Him to jail. He had always been in danger of being put behind bars because of His controversial statements and unconventional methods of working, but as long as I was there, it never happened and I am proud of that It was only after I left the commune were we subjected to the pain and humiliation of seeing Him behind bars.

My abandoning Him created doubts about Him and His power. It was hard to believe for everyone that Bhagwan and I were able to separate. People wondered why I'd left. What was wrong? What had happened? Was there a split between us? Perhaps a power struggle? It raised possibilities for departure for many Sannyasins. He had to stop all this in order to survive.

To address the issue He chose to bury me under sensational accusations and false charges. He awakened dormant, slumbering doubts and negativity about me in everybody. He gave vent to the madness that lay just below the surface of their skin. He killed two birds with one stone: He tested me to the fullest extent and also planted doubts in the minds of His people in order to prevent an exodus.

Everyone believed Him. Everyone participated in His game. A mass rejection of my person was staged. The *Book of Rajneeshism*, which was dictated by Him, a book that detailed the commune's guidelines for the benefit of new Sannyasins was burnt along with my robes of the Rajneesh Academy. I had proudly worn this dress when I was in Rajneeshpuram. It had been designed by Bhagwan. Everyone jumped on the bandwagon and participated in finishing off Sheela. Everyone's destructive streak took possession of them. Even today, no intelligent person can understand the mass hysteria that followed. What was the purpose of this destruction?

As chairman of the Rajneesh Academy, as His secretary, it had been easy for me to preach His teachings. But after His baseless accusations, did I continue doing it? Did I survive in the crossfire of brutal and ugly attacks by Him and His entire commune? Did I stand this painful isolation, the excommunication? Did I live through this hopeless situation? I did. Maybe Bhagwan's teachings gave me the strength.

Perhaps Existence as well as my Khidr wanted to test me, to see if I would be able to survive. I had proven that I was able to care for Him and His people. Now it was time to ascertain whether I was capable of carrying the load of His teaching. He had to cut me off from everybody. He made me the enemy of the whole world. He pushed me into unbearable agony. Hostile conditions were created for me by Him. He offered me a chance to try out all His teachings.

Madness and destruction spread to the whole commune after I left. Any respect for His work, for the work of our master, was very easily lost. It makes no sense. Why did He destroy His own vision in this fit of anger and vengefulness, a vision that I had worked so hard on for six years to bring to life? Why was my good work and respect so easily destroyed and even more quickly forgotten?

He accused me wildly in order to destroy me. He used this strategy to cut Himself off from me. He claimed that He was not aware of how hard His Sannyasins had worked or how hard I had made them work. Eventually He offered all Sannyasins the freedom to do whatever they wanted. They could work if they wanted. They could laze around all day if that's what they wanted. The result was not unexpected. The Sannyasins brought Him to an uncomfortable position. They dived into a whirlpool of claims and complaints. They lost their vigilance. They forgot their responsibility to Him and His people. They became reactionary. They plundered His city, their city, the city that was a living symbol of love and trust. A city that was free of crime and punishment. A city that was always busy with work, music, and laughter. They betrayed His trust. They behaved badly.

He had once said to me about erring Sannyasins: "These are idiots. They will never understand me. They will destroy me and my teachings. They will destroy this commune." And they did.

Freedom does not mean license.

In our Magdalena restaurant, if people were not ready to prepare food claiming they were free and wanted only to meditate, then what is going to happen to five thousand people? What will they eat?

People are not working the way they were working under Sheela. That means you need Sheela. You should be working more — to prove that Sheela's fascism was unnecessary. People are not coming to their work, and even if they come they don't work. Do you see the implication of it?

Five thousand people have to live self-sufficiently. You have to produce your food, your houses, your vegetables, your milk products — everything. And if you are not working, because you think that's what freedom means, then you are behaving stupidly …

(From "Where Do We Go from Here?," in *Osho: From Bondage to Freedom*)

Unfortunately nobody understood this and all was lost.

28
Don't Kill Him:
Respect His teachings and His life

What is respect? One day Bhagwan explained this word to me in a very beautiful way. I had brought Him few drafts of the architectural drawings for the entrance of Rajneesh Mandir Hall and Rajneesh Academy. He asked me what I thought of them.

I replied, "I would like the entrance of Rajneesh Mandir Hall to be something very special. People should turn around to have a second look at it."

He said with a smile, "This is called Respect, Seela. Respect means re-inspect: to have a second look at something. The entrance must be respectful. Your feeling is right, absolutely right."

After my departure from Rajneeshpuram, the Sannyasins lost all respect. They stooped to the level of mass mentality. They plundered the city that they had helped build with so much love—the creation of the man whom they loved. They burned their respect and their spiritual progress together with the Book of Rajneeshism. They forgot meditation and spirituality, provided they had ever possessed them. Common sense was gone. Ordinary decency was lost. They allowed themselves to become a rude, unmannerly crowd.

This must have humiliated Bhagwan more than being thrown out of twenty-one different countries later when nobody wanted Him. He must have longed for a friend in whom He could have confided His grief and pain. He always needed a trustworthy person like me in His proximity. He was a man who had enjoyed the convenience of a trusted devotee and a good manager for years. He was spoiled by my love. His body must have suffered. He must have been ashamed. He must have missed me.

I tell you, He was a proud man. He was proud of His work, of what He had created—perhaps the only successful commune that has ever existed in the whole world.

And, He Himself destroyed it by His vengefulness.

It was very easy to misunderstand Bhagwan. It is always really difficult to understand a man like Him. His way of working was absolutely unconventional. Love and trust were the only foundation on which one could understand and relate to Him. How many of us surrendered unconditionally to Him is a wonder and will remain a question. Even today He remains misunderstood. The world does not understand Him. His own people understand Him even less. That was and is His main misfortune.

Bhagwan was robbed by His own people. And today His Sannyasins are too frightened and ashamed to talk about Rajneeshpuram. In my opinion, His people diminish Him by not talking about this most important time of His life. To erase this phase of His life is to cripple Him. The whole cannot be separated from the part, nor can the part be separated from the whole. Nobody should separate Bhagwan from His creation or His destruction of it. Nobody has the right to do so.

After being rejected from twenty-one countries, Bhagwan returned to India in July 1986. His health kept deteriorating till He died of heart failure three years later. He was only fifty-eight. His ashes are placed in the Poona ashram.

I was in France, close to the German-French border, when I learned about Bhagwan's death. I was living in a small village close to Otmar's home,

One afternoon, around 3:30 p.m., I received a call from Otmar. He was in his office. He had been informed by someone that they had seen on television that Bhagwan had died. Otmar did not believe the information. He called the television station. The information was confirmed. He had then called me immediately to tell me about it.

I was shocked to hear it. Completely in denial. I told Otmar, "It is not possible. It must be a bad joke." Otmar reassured me that he had confirmed this information with the television station and that it was not a joke. Then I said to him, "In that case He has been killed."

Even today I do not accept that it was a natural death. If it was natural I would have certainly felt it.

I have missed Him every day since then. His beautiful face, the special touch of His hand and feet, His charming voice, His madness—I have missed it all. I have never stopped loving Him and never will.

The censorship and rituals which are performed by

the Sannyasins now after His death are totally against His life, death, and teachings. His discourses as Bhagwan Shree Rajneesh were divine, even if some of His actions as a fallible human being were flawed. In order to be complete, history needs to note both. There is no need to rewrite, revise history. These empty rituals kill Him. Please stop them. His soul left His body in 1990. Now, please, Don't Kill Him!

MEMORIES

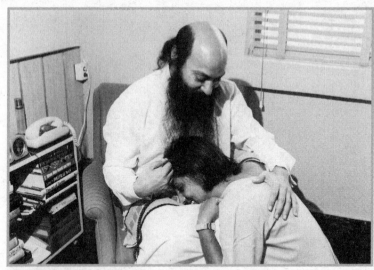
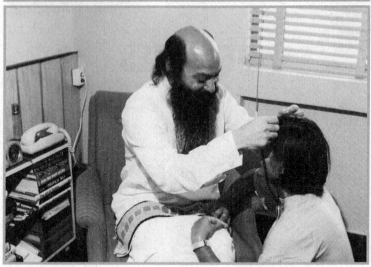

Above and Below: Bhagwan and I in His Woodlands apartment in Bombay; 1973.

My treasured moments with Bhagwan. This was clicked on one of
my afternoon visits with Bhagwan in front of His room in Mt Abu;
1973.

Above: In *darshan* with Bhagwan in Poona; 1980. One would be compelled to surrender completely in His presence.

Below: Assisting Bhagwan in *darshan* as His secretary in the Poona Ashram.

Guru Purnima celebrations at a meditation camp in Mt Abu; 1973.

Above, Below, and Adjacent: Bhagwan and I at the immigration office in Portland.

Bhagwan and I greeting the Sannyasin workers of the Krishnamurti Dam, in Rajneeshpuram.

Above and Below: Working with Bhagwan. I used to work with Him for hours on end. He would give me directives about everything in detail. Though it was exhausting, I always enjoyed working hard.

In a meeting during my official visit to Sweden in 1983. Sweden was a dry country; alcohol was available in the state only at a very high price. So I thought it would be a funny gift to present alcohol at the meeting. No one expects alcohol from a religious person. Before my meeting I hid the bottles in my belt under my cape. I began the meeting by taking off my cape. The whole room with 250-300 people burst into laughter immediately. Alcohol was not a taboo in our community. To be unaware was a taboo.

Bhagwan often spoke about the seriousness of established religions. In His opinion, religion should be full of fun and laughter, and that is exactly how I understood religion from Bhagwan.

Above and Below: Promoting Rajneeshism in Sweden. It was important for us to be a religion for immigration purposes. Bhagwan's visa as a religious leader could not be valid unless He had a religion. That is why He created Rajneeshism. Here I am addressing a crowd in Sweden as Bhagwan's personal secretary. Bhagwan had specially designed this outfit for me.

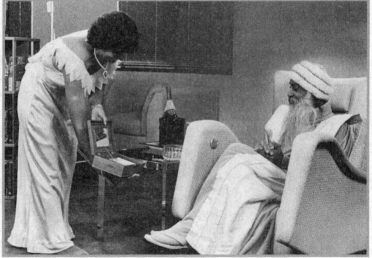

Above: Bhagwan showing me the Rolls-Royce He had Himself bought in my absence; at Kip's Castle, New Jersey.

Below: A lover was always greeted at my house with a bottle of champagne and Habana cigars. Here, I am offering Bhagwan Habana cigars; in Rajneeshpuram.

Above: Bhagwan, Vivek, and my then husband Jay on an afternoon drive in New Jersey with me.

Below: Bhagwan at my Rajneeshpuram house in 1983. He'd come for an interview with journalists. This picture was clicked right after He made a funny comment in response to a question. He was very witty and clever with His remarks. These often created trouble for us though.

Above: I am conducting a meeting with Sannyasins in Rajneeshpuram
Below: I had organized a stylish party at my house in Rajneeshpuram for important business people and some politicians of Oregon during our early days at the Big Muddy Ranch. We wanted to show these important people that we were as normal as they were.

Above: Bhagwan on one of his drive by in Rajnesshpuram
Below: Me in my Rajneeshpuram finery.

Note from the German Translator, Susanna Christinck

Under normal circumstances, this book would have never been able to emerge. But the circumstances were not normal and neither is this book. It was written by Sheela within a few weeks, in the time she took out of her everyday work. She offered me to live in her home during the translation of the book. I was happy to accept this generous invitation. So it happened that for a few weeks I stayed at her private home for the young, the old, the disabled, and all those in need of care. During this stay, I got to know Sheela's life.

Already during my first visit I had been touched by the way she received anybody who entered her home. Everyone is welcome there, no matter how old he is, what language she speaks, or what background they have. Be it Sannyasins or non-Sannyasins, be it relatives of her patrons or handymen, she talks to everyone personally. Every person is touched by her warmth.

For weeks I saw how Sheela gets up early in the morning daily, how she showers her patients, dresses them, and helps them with breakfast. Almost always she prepares the meals herself. She also takes great care to serve the food to the old people and to her employees herself. She goes shopping, feeds her patients, and is always available when someone needs something.

With absolute certainty she comes to know when one has worries or problems. Her humour and contentment are contagious. In her presence, it seems easy for everyone to forget their problems and the seriousness of their lives, and to simply find joy in the present.

Sheela always has an open ear for the relatives of her patients. She listens to their worries and talks to them. If somebody's approaching death weighs heavy on the family members, she gives them comfort and confidence. Her ordinary workday is from dawn until late at night; she knows no breaks and, if necessary, she continues even after midnight.

When she was writing this book, some very unexpected incidents and disasters occurred. Her mother, who had just come from India, had a heart attack. A patient in her home died. In his last days he had needed more care than usual, and after his death a considerable amount of bureaucratic and organizational effort was also required.

As if this was not enough, her beloved rabbit Dumdum, also called Hasi, died soon. He was as much a part of her family as were others who lived there. Dumdum was a very special rabbit. He lived in complete freedom, ran through the house, visited the patients in their rooms, and gave a lot of joy to everyone. Among his special qualities was to lie at night as a watchdog before Sheela's room and make loud noises if anyone approached. He was always available for her, probably more than any human could ever be. Visitors also had fun with him. This beautiful creature contributed a lot to the atmosphere and beauty of her home.

Despite all these unexpected events, Sheela could not be prevented from continuously writing this book. This allowed me to get an idea of how she must have created a wonderful living space for nearly five thousand people in Oregon from scratch. I have seen with my own eyes how she blithely pursues her goals despite all obstacles, how she strives to meet the needs of everybody before thinking of herself. All situations, all events, even the most unpleasant ones, are suffered by her with complete serenity and acceptance, because for her it is not a theory but a fact that all situations are given to her by Existence.

So, this book took shape within a very short time and under relatively unconventional circumstances. Other authors need years to accomplish such a work. But Sheela is not a woman of big words. Much more important for her are actions. They are the essence of what one has learned.

This book is also an essence, the essence of her life with Bhagwan. Sheela's life with him by no means finished with their physical separation. As I understand it, for her there is no difference between her life during her time with Bhagwan in Bombay, Pune, or Rajneeshpuram and her current life. She has always cared for people and their needs. Erstwhile it was Bhagwan's people, today it's her own people.

What is incomprehensible for me is how did some people, especially Sannyasins, behave with her back then and still do today. I cannot understand how the image that many people still have of Sheela was ever created. While working on this book I experienced first-hand how the existing community of Sannyasins, be it the commune in Pune or other similar institutions, is still very hostile towards her. They still cherish totally unjustified prejudices. This was clearly shown by the fact that information and generally available publications of Bhagwan were deliberately held back and made unavailable when it was realized that Sheela wanted to do something with them. The mere mention of her name is sufficient to spark and ignite any of these supposedly peaceful Sannyasins.

Of course, I can dismiss all this as coincidence, but that would be too easy. The impression remains that a large part of Bhagwan's followers carry massive prejudices against Sheela. Even the official press policy of the commune in Pune is influenced by this. Information related to Bhagwan's commune in America is held back. Summaries of Bhagwan's life are issued as official press releases in which this important period in Bhagwan's life is not mentioned at all. The impression that's given is that there was only one commune in Pune. The most important and the greatest work of his life is not mentioned at all.

This incomplete summary of Bhagwan's life is also contained in many of his books. For the current leaders of the Pune commune the time in America is like a red flag. They don't want to be confronted with it. I think this is a shame. In my understanding, Bhagwan placed greater emphasis on absolute openness than anyone else before him. This includes not sweeping unpleasant events under the cover. One should stand courageously for one's own actions. This trait is obviously not present in many of his current supporters.

I fail to understand how these people can justify this to themselves. They call themselves disciples of Bhagwan and, at the same time, they don't want to look at the reality of his life. And it is not only the Sannyasins who think that Sheela has committed grave crimes, a huge part of the public opinion also seems to be convinced that it's prudent to remain as far as possible from Sheela.

Her entry into Germany is still denied. The reason given is that she was in jail in the US and ex-convicts can be refused entry without explanation by the German authorities. Behind such an approach there must, however, be other reasons.

When her entry was first prohibited, she just wanted to cross the border to Germany together with a mate who had been in prison with her for the same charges. Her friend was not denied entry. This apparent arbitrariness may be due to the fact that the German authorities are perhaps still afraid that Sheela may once again build a Rajneeshpuram.

Since her release Sheela has continuously worked on improving the living conditions of the needy and creating a decent living environment for them. This is an issue which is as important in Germany as it is in Switzerland and will be brought into light more and more in the coming years. The creative work that Sheela does in the field of care for the elderly would certainly be advantageous in more ways than one for Germany. Various German agencies spend a huge sum every year on old-age issues, but these expenses do not guarantee the old a decent life. Sheela's home is the answer to the unbearable isolation and coldness of nursing homes. Her home is a model institution which demonstrates how people needing care can live together in a family-like atmosphere.

For me it is just amazing how well Sheela managed to stuck to Bhagwan's teachings in her daily life despite all the obstacles that were placed in her way. Without a spiritual claim, without any theoretical concepts, she brings life, love, and laughter into her home. This is noticeable to everyone. In my eyes, Sheela is a living example that real growth has nothing to do with spiritual ideologies or modern education. It must take place in the heart of every person and can be realized anytime, anywhere.

Susanna Christinck translated the original
text from English to German

Chronology

December 11, 1931: Bhagwan Shree Rajneesh is born as Chandra Mohan Jain in Kuchwada, a small village in Madhya Pradesh, Central India.

December 28, 1949: Ma Anand Sheela is born in Baroda, India, as Sheela Ambalal Patel.

March 21, 1953: Bhagwan Rajneesh becomes enlightened at the age of twenty-one under a Maulshree tree in Jabalpur.

1956: Bhagwan receives His MA in Philosophy from the University of Sagar, Madhya Pradesh.

1957-1966: Bhagwan works as a university professor, first for a brief while at Raipur Sanskrit College, then for a longer time at the Jabalpur University. He also travels through India giving discourses in various cities and towns.

1962: First meditation centers, called Jeevan Jagruti Kendras, come up in various cities across the country.

1968-1970: *From Sex to Superconsciouness* published. Bhagwan Rajneesh begins to be called "Sex Guru."

April 14th, 1970: Bhagwan introduces His revolutionary meditation technique, Dynamic Meditation.

September 26, 1970: Bhagwan initiates His first group of disciples into neo-Sannyas in a meditation camp on the foothills of Himalayas.

December 1970: Bhagwan moves into the Woodlands Apartments in Bombay and stays there till March 1974. During this time, He regularly holds public lectures and meditation camps.

May 1971: Bhagwan changes His name from Acharya Shree Rajneesh to Bhagwan Shree Rajneesh and, for the first time, publicly acknowledges that He is enlightened.

March 21, 1974: Bhagwan moves to Koregaon Park in Pune.

July 1974-April 1981: Bhagwan gives discourses every morning in the Poona ashram.

August 1975: The first therapy groups begin. Their violent and sexual nature generates negative press.

May 22, 1980: Vilas Tupe, a member of a fundamentalist Hindu group, throws a knife at Bhagwan Rajneesh during His morning discourse. The assassination attempt fails, and Tupe is taken into custody.

January, 1981: Ma Sheela Anand is officially appointed as Bhagwan's secretary.

April 10, 1981: Bhagwan enters a three-and-a-half-year period of self-imposed public silence.

June 1, 1981: Bhagwan flies from Bombay to New York with His household and medical staff.

July 10, 1981: Ma Sheela purchases the 64,000-acre Big Muddy Ranch to create Rajneeshpuram.

August-October 1984: Salmonella outbreak in The Dalles, Oregon; 751 people affected, no casualties.

October 30, 1984: Bhagwan breaks His vow of silence after 1315 days; starts speaking to small groups in His residence.

July 1985: He starts giving public discourses every morning to thousands of seekers in Rajneesh Mandir.

September 14, 1985: Ma Sheela resigns and leaves Rajneesh-puram. Other members of her team follow in her footsteps the next day.

September 16, 1985: Bhagwan holds a press conference in which He accuses Ma Sheela and her associates of having committed a number of serious crimes, most of these dating back to 1984, and invites the authorities to investigate.

October 23, 1985: A federal grand jury issues a thirty-five-count indictment charging Bhagwan Rajneesh and several other Sannyasins with conspiracy to evade immigration laws.

October 28, 1985: Bhagwan and a small number of Sannyasins accompanying Him are arrested aboard a rented Learjet at a North Carolina airstrip. In West Germany, Ma Sheela is also arrested; she is extradited to the US.

December 1985: Bhagwan returns to India with His new secretary and other western disciples. But when the visas of the non-Indians in his team are revoked, Bhagwan leaves the country.

July 29, 1986: After either being deported or denied entry in twenty-one countries, Bhagwan returns to India.

January 4, 1987: Bhagwan moves back to the Poona Ashram.

December 1988: Ma Sheela is released for good behaviour after serving thirty-nine months of the fifty-four month sentence.

February 29, 1989: The disciples of Bhagwan Shree Rajneesh collectively decide to call Him "Osho Rajneesh."

January 19, 1990: Bhagwan dies, reportedly of heart failure. His ashes are placed in the Poona Ashram. His epitaph reads:

OSHO
Never Born
Never Died
Only Visited this
Planet Earth between
December 11 1931 – January 19 1990